IRAN

H e who would come with me to see Esfahan in the
beautiful May sun can expect long walks in the
burning sun, in the bitter cold winds of the highest altitudes,
across these Asian plateaus, the highest and most immense
on earth, the cradle of humanity.

Pierre Loti

Translated from the French by Claire Parker
Copy editor: Kirk McElhearn

Technical and Artistic Director:
Ahmed-Chaouki Rafif

Assistant:
Yves Korbendau

Editorial and Iconographic Coordination:
Marie-Pierre Kerbrat

© 2002, ACR Édition Internationale, Courbevoie (Paris)
(Art - Création - Réalisation)
ISBN 2-86770-153-8
N° d'éditeur 1154
Dépôt légal : premier trimestre 2002

Printed in France by Mame in Tours

Yves Korbendau

The Many Faces of
IRAN

ACR Edition

CONTENTS

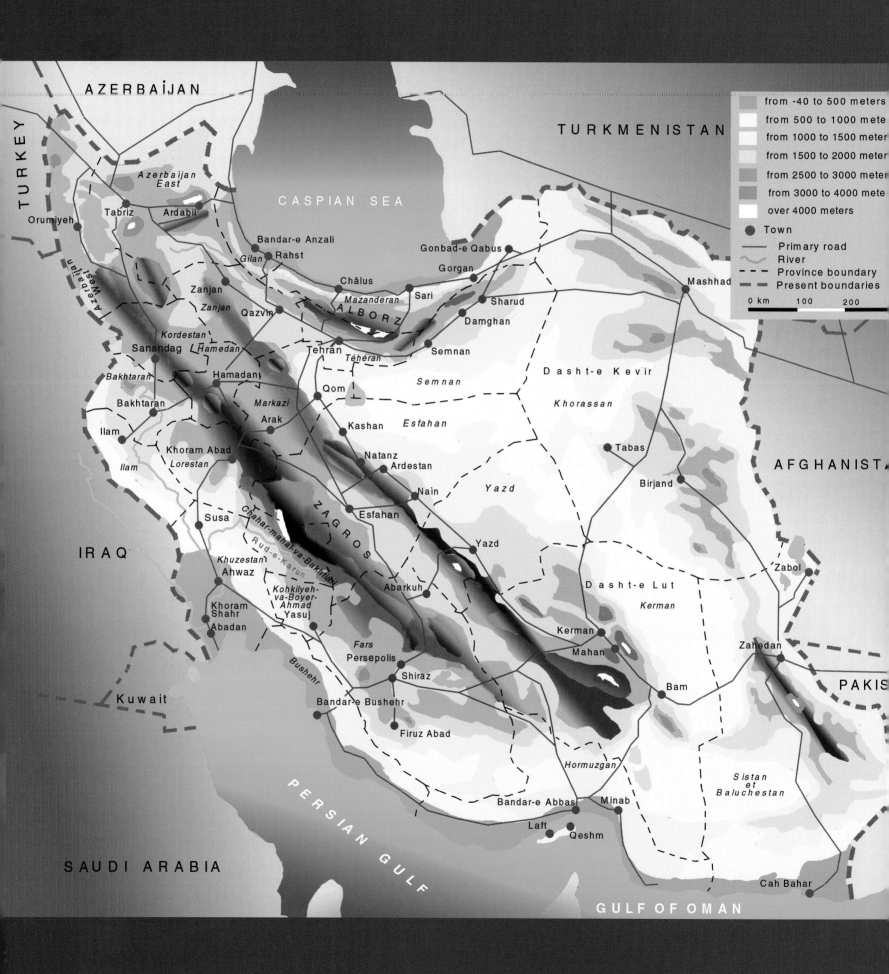

THE HISTORY OF IRAN TIMELINE

Tho History of Iran - timeline

YEAR	PERIOD	WORLD EVENTS	EVENTS IN IRAN
BC	PRIMITIVE IRAN		Agricultural peoples Remarkable pottery swords, bronze daggers and tablets appear
5th and 4th millennia		EGYPT Ancient Empire Pyramids at Geysa	--------
2700-2300			Apogee of SUMERIAN civilisation
24th century	ANCIENT IRAN		-------- first dynasty of ELAM
1900		Mesopotamia	
1300		First Assyrian Empire	Empire of ELAM Ziggurat
1146		Renaissance of Assyria NEBUCHADREZZAR I	-------- capital at Susa
7th century			-------- The MEDES occupy the plain of Ecbatana
550-331			-------- PERSIAN Empire Achaemenids
558-528			CYRUS II the Great
522-486			DARIUS I
509		Roman Republic	
500			
490		The Greeks defeat the Persians at Marathon	
480		Greek victory at Salamis	XERXES I
486-465			
465-424		Fall of the Athenian Empire	ARTAXERXES I
404			
404-358			ARTAXERXES II
356-323		Alexander the Great invades Persia	--------
312-64			Hellenistic period SELEUCIDS after the death of Alexander the Great
300		Fall of CARTHAGE	--------
250			The PARTHIANS
171-138			MITHRADATES I
49-44		Caesar's dictatorship	
56-37			Reign of ORODES
25		AUGUSTUS Roman Emperor	Apogee of Parthian power
A.D.			
23-40		CALIGULA Roman Emperor	
37-41		CLAUDIUS Roman Emperor	Revolt within the Empire

PRINCIPAL SITES

UR
Mesopotamia

CHOGA-ZANBIL

SUSA

HAMADAN

PERSEPOLIS

Takes control of Susa
and Persepolis

Capital at Antioch

Capital at Ctesiphon
close to Baghdad

Ziggurat CHOGA-ZANBIL

PASARGADAE

SUSA

CTESIPHON

PERSEPOLIS

YEAR	PERIOD	WORLD EVENTS	EVENTS IN IRAN
224-651	PRE - ISLAMIC IRAN		SASSANIAN Empire
224-241			ARDASHIR I
241-272			SHAPUR I
309-379			SHAPUR II
330		Constantinople capital of the Roman Empire	
363			Victory of Shapur II over the Emperor Julian
383-388			SHAPUR III
399-420			YAZDAGIRD I
414		The Visigoths in Spain	
457-484			FIRUZ I
481-511		Clovis King of France	
531-579			KHOSROW I takes over the cities of
570		Birth of Mohammed	
578			Apogee of the SASSANIAN Empire
590-628			KHOSROW II establishes new borders
622		Flight of Mohammed to Medina Beginning of the HEGIRA	The Persians against the Byzantine Empire
626			
632-651			YAZDAGIRD III
631	ISLAMIC IRAN	Death of the Prophet Mohammed	End of the Sassanian dynasty at the battle of Nehavand --------
651-750			UMAYYAD CALIPHATE
680		Death of the Imam Hossein at Kerbala	--------
732		Victory of Charles Martel over the Saracens at Poitiers	
750-1258			ABBASSID CALIPHATE
751-987		Carolingians in France	--------
768-814		Reign of Charlemagne	DYNASTIES
820-873			TAHARIDS
862-900			SAFARIS
900-999			SAMANIDS
928-1077			ZYARIDS
935-1055			BUYIDS

PRINCIPAL SITES

FIRUZ ABAD

NAQSH-E RADJAB

NAQSH-E ROSTAM

TAKHT-E SOLEIMAN

ANTIOCH
BYZANTIUM

JERUSALEM, DAMASCUS
EGYPT

CONSTANTINOPLE

close to HAMADAN

FIRUZ ABAD

NAQSH-E RADJAB

NAQSH-E ROSTAM

TAKHT-E
SOLEIMAN

YEAR	PERIOD	WORLD EVENTS	EVENTS IN IRAN
962-1040	MIDDLE AGES		GHAZNAVIDS
1000-1157			SELJUKS
1149-1209			GHORIDS
1187		Jerusalem taken by SALADIN	
1221			Invasion by GENGIS KHAN
1256-1334			MONGOLS
1370-1502			TIMURIDS
1492	MODERN ERA	GRANADA lost	
1502-1722			SAFAVIDS
1515		FRANCOIS I MARIGNAN	
1524-1576			Shah TAHMASP
1526		BABUR the Great Moghol Emperor of India	
1587-1628			Shah ABBAS I
1643-1715		Reign of LOUIS XIV	DYNASTIES
1715		Reign of LOUIS XV	
1750-1799	CONTEMPORARY ERA		ZENDS
1786-1925			QADJAR
1789		States General and French revolution	capital transferred to
1804		NAPOLEON I Emperor of France	
1859		SUEZ canal built	
1914-1918		World War I	
1925-1979			PAHLAVIS
1925-1941			REZA SHAH PAHLAVI
1939-1945		World War II	
1941-1979			MOHAMED REZA SHAH PAHLAVI
1951			Oil nationalised
1/2/1979			Return of AYATOLLAH KHOMEINY
1/4/1979			Proclamation of the ISLAMIC REPUBLIC of IRAN
9/1980-7/1988			Iran-Iraq war
4/6/1989			Death of AYATOLLAH KHOMEINY

TABRIZ
capital

QAZVIN
capital

ESFAHAN
capital in 1598

SHIRAZ
capital

TEHRAN
capital

QAZVIN
Tchehel Sotun Palace

ESFAHAN
Mosque of the Imam

SHIRAZ
Karim Khan Zend

TEHRAN
Golestan Palace

TEHRAN
Azadi Tower

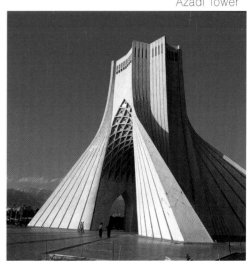

AZERBAİJAN

TURKMENISTAN

CASPIAN SEA

TURKEY

Orumiyeh lake

MEDIA

ALBORZ

PARTHIA

Turang tépé

Tépé Hisar

KHORASAN

Dasht-e Kevir

Ecbatana
Hamadan

Kangavar
Bakhtaran
Bisotun

Gandj-e Nameh

LORESTAN

AFGHANISTAN

SUSIANA

Susa

Choqa
Zanbil

ZAGROS

Rud-e-Karun

IRAQ

KHUZITAN

Dasht-e Lut

Our

PERSIA

Persépolis
Pasargadae

PAKIST

Naqsh-e Bostam

Kuwait

FARS

SAUDI ARABIA

PERSIAN GULF

GULF OF OMAN

from -40 to 500 meters
from 500 to 1000 meter
from 1000 to 1500 meters
from 1500 to 2000 meters
from 2500 to 3000 meters
from 3000 to 4000 meter
over 4000 meters

● Elamite or Mede site
● Achaemenid site
● Seleucid or Parthian sit
- - Present boundaries

0 km   100   200   3

ANCIENT IRAN

The Empire of Elam

The Medes
The Achaemenids
The Seleucids
The Parthian Empire

The earliest traces of civilisation have been found bordering the Zagros Mountains along the Mesopotamian basin. Excavations have revealed elements that go back to the Neolithic age (4000 BC). The discovery of articles of pottery has enabled archaeologists to uncover drawings that provide clues about these peoples who worked the land.

Scythian jewellery found at Tepe Hissar close to Damghan and Mycenian tombs and vases shows that new populations from various regions made incursions into this territory.

In the fourth millennium BC, Susiana was dominated by Sumer. In the third millennium, the history of the Iranian Plateau began with the Elamites. They established their capital at Awan (north-west of Susa) and were subject to attacks from king Sargon, the former sovereign of the Akkad dynasty, around 2400 BC.

The apogee of the **kingdom of Elam**, whose borders extended from the banks of the Tigris to Persepolis, was under the reign of Shilkhak-In-Shushinak (1151-1065 BC). Nebuchadrezzar I (1146-1123 BC), king of Babylon, then succeeded once more in dominating the region.

There was then a long period of silence until six **Mede** tribes decided to join forces and form a nation under Dieoces (708-655 BC), who established the capital at Ecbatana (Hamadan). They seized Nineveh in 606 BC during the reign of Cyaxares (633-584 BC), which provoked the decline of Assyria. The new Mede king Astyages had a peaceful reign, but in 558 BC, Cyrus II (founder of the **Achaemenid** dynasty) defeated his overlord and subjugated all of Media. He expanded his kingdom and reigned from the Indus to the Aegean. His eldest son, Cambyses (530-522 BC) succeeded him and seized Egypt. Darius I (522-486 BC), known as "Darius the Great", organised his empire into twenty-three provinces. He colonised Thrace and Macedonia but was defeated by the Greeks at Marathon (490 BC). Xerxes I continued to battle against the Greeks; he eliminated Leonidas at Thermopylae, and seized and burned Athens, but his fleet was annihilated at Salamis.

The empire was sustained through the peaceful reigns of three sovereigns, then began to disintegrate, and, despite the efforts of Artaxerxes III (358-338), Persia was conquered by the armies of Alexander the Great (356-323).

The Macedonian general Seleucus founded the **Seleucid** dynasty, created new towns in Susiana and maintained the peace in his states. His successors were unable to prevent the splintering of this empire. The states freed themselves, and the **Parthians** (a people of Iranian origin that lived between the Caspian and Aral Seas) claimed their independence.

Mithradates I (171-138) took Media, Fars, Elam and Babylon, and extended the Parthian empire from the Euphrates to Herat. The apogee of Parthian power was under the reign of Orodes (56-37). His fall was not due to the constant combat with the Romans, which had been going on for two centuries, but to internal rivalries. A new dynasty then took over.

CHOGA - ZANBIL

The Empire of Elam flourished in Mesopotamia from the third millennium BC. The best example of a ziggurat from this period is found close to Susa, near the Iraqi border. It was built by king Untash-Napirisha in the 13th century BC in the centre of his religious capital. It had five floors and must have been around 60 m high. At the summit, a temple was dedicated to the king of Susa. Despite the passage of time, it is still 25 m high with three well-preserved floors.

The different levels can be reached via a monumental staircase to a platform with a commanding view of the surrounding desert.

A number of baked bricks still bear readable inscriptions.

PASARGADAE

Cyrus II the Great, founder of the Persian Achaemenid dynasty, chose to establish his capital at Pasargadae in 539 BC. The only remains of the royal residence are the stone slabs of the main hall, surrounded by column bases and a few bas-reliefs (see right): the so-called Cyrus stele, representing a protective genie, a head crowned with a tiara, and the lower body of a bull.

The tomb of Cyrus (below) is impressive due to the huge size of the construction materials used. Its full height of 10.7 m, the nature of the white limestone and the sober lines make it an impressive sight, particularly at sunset

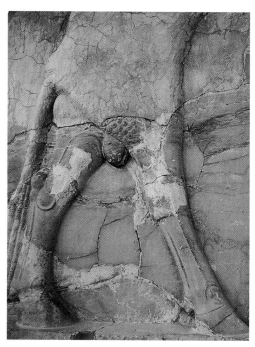

Darius I, who succeeded Cyrus II, preferred to transfer his capital to Persepolis, on a defensive site on the Marv-e Dasht plain, as he considered Pasargadae to be too exposed.

This palace was especially designed to lavishly celebrate No Ruz (New Year), when the representatives of the twenty-eight nations (vassal states) came to offer their gifts to the powerful Achaemenid sovereign. The procession climbed the monumental staircase to reach the Apadana (above), the reception hall where the king received gifts from the Medes and the Susians, furs from Sogdiana, gold powder from India and dromedaries from Arabia.

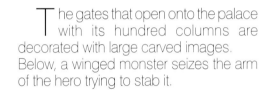

Darius's palace, adjacent to the Apadana, is surrounded by doors decorated with bas-reliefs representing the king fighting a lion, a bull and a chimera. The southeast staircase is decorated with guards and vassals.

The gates that open onto the palace with its hundred columns are decorated with large carved images. Below, a winged monster seizes the arm of the hero trying to stab it.

A series of figures appear to be climbing up either side of the small north staircase leading to the Tripylon (previous pages).
The lines of warriors all look identical. There is nothing unusual about this. We can admire the variety and sophistication of the costumes, headdresses and gifts borne by the figures in the processions of gift bearers from far-off lands the Persians had conquered.

Above left, a Persian officer is facing a Mede officer, recognisable by his round headdress.

24

P e r s e p o l i s

A succession of dignitaries and Persian and Mede officers make up the procession to swear allegiance to the Achaemenid sovereign for the No Ruz celebrations.
These bas-reliefs were finely carved in black marble from the Majdarab Mountains. The lips and clothes of some figures were coloured.

The Mede officer places his hand in front of his mouth as a sign of respect when he addresses his sovereign (next page).

The representations of the different figures we can see on the façades of the staircases leading to the Apadana give us an idea of the scale of the celebrations that took place in this sumptuous palace. These perfectly preserved representations show us the diversity of the peoples through their clothing and headdresses. A great number of peoples are represented: Persians, Bablyonians, Medes, Parthians, Cilicians, Scythians, Assyrians, Chorasmians from Central Asia, Ethiopians, Egyptians, Cappadocians, Somalians, Ionians, Arabs, Thracians, etc.

Gifts of all kinds are shown in this procession. For example, we can see people from Central Asia with rams, natives from the Indus carrying flasks that are probably filled with gold in baskets, and camels driven by nomads from Central Asia.
The Persian and Mede soldiers march stiffly and their silhouettes are often similar. The tribute-bearers show a much wider variety of detail.

The story that Persepolis was destroyed in 330 BC, by Alexander the Great under the influence of his mistress Thaïs and of copious wine served at a feast, is probably simply a legend.
Alexander the Great definitely annihilated Persepolis to take revenge for the Persian invasion of Greece. The palace was pillaged several times. According to historians, there are no traces of fire, and few objects have been found during excavations.

NAQSH-E ROSTAM

The tombs of four Achaemenid kings were dug into the high cliff of Kuh-e Hussein, 5 km to the north of Persepolis. The tomb of Darius I (above right) was the first of this kind carved into the rock with inscriptions in cuneiform characters and in the Persian, Elamite and Babylonian languages. The tombs of Xerxes I and Artaxerxes I are found on the same face (on the left). The tomb of Darius II was sculpted on the other side (next page, detail on the bottom right). There are interesting bas-reliefs sculpted on the upper part representing conquered peoples supporting the king, and god Ahura Mazda on a platform.

BISOTUN

Darius I had this memorial sculpted in 520 BC to commemorate his victory over the magus Gaumatas after fighting nineteen battles against him.

He chose this location at an elevation of around sixty metres on the royal way leading from Babylon to Ecbatana (Hamadan) in order to reach all those under his power. The bas-relief shows, on the left, the king of kings crushing his enemy with his foot, and in front of him the eight rebel princes chained to one another.

A text in three languages (Babylonian, Elamite and Persian) tells of the combat so that future generations would hear his message.

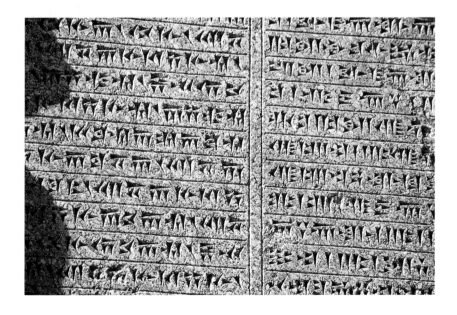

The site of Gandj-e Nameh ("book of treasure") at the foot of Mount Elvend is a beautiful dale whose waterways and waterfalls radiate coolness.

Two large inscriptions are carved into the mass of rock 200 m high.

The left-hand inscription is attributed to Darius the Great and the other to his son Xerxes. Both texts are written in Old Persian, Neo-Elamite and Neo-Babylonian. They are almost identical. The only difference is in the names of the genealogies. They both praise the god who created the world, Ahura Mazda, and list the titles of the king of kings.

HAMADAN

Xerxes (485-465 BC) apparently married a Jewish woman named Esther. She sent for her uncle Mardocai to organise the Jewish colony that was under the king's protection. The mausoleum where the queen was laid to rest is a small building with a brick dome above a vestibule.

Inside, two cenotaphs in carved ebony are covered in drapes. Esther's is on the right. History also attributes this mausoleum to the Jewish queen Yezdedgerd I (399), wife of the Sassanian king.

The small town of Kangavar is located halfway between Hamadan and Bakhtaran (Kermanshah).

Nothing remains of the hill but the ruins of a temple, dedicated to Anahita, goddess of waters and fertility, built during the Seleucid or Parthian era.

Iranian archaeologists have excavated the remains of a monumental double staircase. The staircase resembles those at the Apadana in Persepolis.

The foundations of the temple and the bases of the huge columns are similar to those found in Greece.

AZERBAÏJAN

TURKEY

TURKMENISTAN

	from -40 to 500 meters
	from 500 to 1000 meters
	from 1000 to 1500 meters
	from 1500 to 2000 meters
	from 2500 to 3000 meters
	from 3000 to 4000 meters
	over 4000 meters
●	Sassanian site
- - -	Present boundaries

0 km   100   200   30

CASPIAN SEA

Nev Shapur

Takht-e Soleiman

ALBORZ

KHORASSAN

Damghan

MÉDIA

Dasht-e Kevir

Nehavand

Qom

Taq-e Bostam

Kashan

Natanz

AFGHANISTA

ZAGROS

Esfahan

Yazd

IRAQ

KERMAN

Dasht-e Lut

Nasqh-e Radjab

Kazerun

Djerre

Naqsh-e Rostam

PAKIST

Kuwait

FARS

Sarvestan

Gur   Darabgird

Firuz Abad

PERSIAN GULF

SAUDI ARABIA

GULF OF OMAN

PRE-ISLAMIC IRAN

THE SASSANIANS

2 2 4 - 6 5 1

In his Book of Kings, "Shahnameh", the poet Ferdowsi wrote: "Centuries passed when it seemed as though there was not a king on earth." The entire Orient was under the influence of Greece.

However, in the region of Fars, traditions had been maintained, and the ambition of Ardashir I (224-241) of the Sassan family was to restore the power of the Achaemenids. He had his princely palace built at Gur (Firuz-Abad). In 224, he attacked and killed his overlord Artaban V, and was crowned "King of the Kings of Iran". Conquest after conquest ensued, and a new Iranian empire, which stretched from Babylonia to Afghanistan, rivalled the power of the Roman Empire.

Shapur I (241-272) fought Rome and took Emperor Valerian prisoner (260). For several centuries, sovereigns succeeded one another, and the battle against the Romans continued.

A new enemy from Central Asia, the Hephtalite Huns, attacked Persia in the 5th century. They weren't driven back until the reign of Khosrow I (531-579). This was the apogee of the Sassanian Empire, which extended as far as Byzantium and Yemen.

Twelve kings succeeded one another in the space of five years, and the power base disintegrated. The last king, Yazdagird III (632-651) attempted to resist, but his territories and strongholds were taken by the Caliphate armies.

The Sassanian Empire, which dominated Iran for four centuries (224-651), was based on a state religion and a rigid hierarchy where the king was almost considered as a god, flanked by important dignitaries and religious leaders. The clergy, who were extremely powerful, ensured that the state religion was respected. While the only remains of buildings from this era are ruins, the Sassanian monarchs left representations of great moments in their history on well-preserved bas-reliefs that can be seen at Taq-e Bostan, Naqsh-e Rostam and Naqsh-e Rajab.

Taq-e Bostan, an important Sassanian site located 12 km from Bakhtaran (Kermanshah) at the foot of a cliff, is situated in pleasant surroundings, with a garden and a pond fed by a spring. A first panel sculpted in bas-relief (below left) represents the investiture of Ardashir II (379-383). To his right, the god Hormuzd presents him with rings tied with ribbons, the symbol of royalty, and to his left, the god Mithra holds out the sacred bundle of twigs, the "barsom".

A small distance away are two man-made caves. The principal cave has the most beautiful bas-reliefs (previous page). In the upper half, the god Ahura Mazda is investing Khosrow II. Behind him, we can see Anahita, the goddess of waters. Underneath, king Khosrow II, dressed in a helmet and chain mail, sword and shield in hand, sits astride his charger Chabdiz. On the side walls, magnificent finely-carved sculptures illustrate hunting scenes (next page).

E ight bas-reliefs illustrate the Sassanian epic. Below the Achaemenid sepulchres, we can see the investiture of the king Narses by the goddess Anahita (previous page, under the photograph of the site), the Roman Emperor Valerian (previous page) taken prisoner at the battle of Edessa in 260 AD following the victory of Shapur I, the investiture of Ardashir I (224-241), founder of the dynasty (above) and the god Ahura Mazda on horseback facing him. Below is the Ka'ba Zadusht, the temple of standards.

At a grandiose site, an old shallow volcano crater is filled with a lake of an intense blue. This site was a major religious centre for the Sassanians where the "warrior's fire" burned. In the Parthian period, the big circular wall was made of unglazed brick. The Sassanians rebuilt it in stone, and reinforced it with twenty-eight bastions and a monumental gate that is still almost intact. All that remains of the temples are ruins.

TAKHT-E SOLEIMAN

NAQSH-E RADJAB

C lose to Persepolis, on the flanks of the Kuh-e Rahmat, three Sassanian bas-reliefs represent two investiture scenes: that of Shapur I (241-272) and that of Ardashir I (224-241), and Shapur on horseback (above), escorted by his noble guards and foot soldiers.

The remains of an ancient Sassanian bridge lie on the road from Shiraz to Firuz-Abad (opposite).

The ancient town of Gur, one of the most important towns under the Sassanians, is found 120 km south of Shiraz, close to Firuz-Abad.

The palace, built by Ardashir I in 224 AD, is an interesting architectural example, with an entrance iwan and a large 13.30 m square hall. This is doubtless one of the first buildings made with a square base topped with a circular cupola. At the start of the Islamic era, mosques were of the Arab type imported and imposed upon Iran. Later, monuments like this palace enabled the Iranian mosque to be created with an iwan and square halls covered with cupolas and domes. A few banks of earth prove that ramparts surrounded the town.

AZERBAİJAN

TURKMENISTAN

TURKEY

CASPIAN SEA

from -40 to 500 meters
from 500 to 1000 meters
from 1000 to 1500 meters
from 1500 to 2000 meters
from 2500 to 3000 meters
from 3000 to 4000 meters
over 4000 meters
● Islamic site
- - - Present boundaries

0 km   100   200   300

Tabriz
Orumieyeh lake
Ardabil

Gonbad-e Qavus
Gorgan
KHORASSAN

Mashhad

Soltanieh
Alumut
MAZANDARAN
Bastam

ALBORZ
Qazvin
Damghan

Tehran
Semnan

Dasht-e Kevir

Hamadan

Qom

Kashan
Natanz
Zavareh
LORESTAN
Ardestan
AFGHANISTA

Nain

KHUZISTAN
Esfahan
Susa
ZAGROS
Yazd
Fahraj

Shuhstar
Rud-e-Karun
IRAQ
Abarkuh
KERMAN

Dasht-e Lut

Kerman
PAKIST

Mahan

Kuwait
Shiraz
Bam

SAUDI ARABIA

PERSIAN GULF

GULF OF OMAN

ISLAMIC IRAN

After the death of Mohammed in 632, the Caliphs led the Islamic world. Yazdagird III, the last Sassanian sovereign, could not hold out against the Arab armies, and the Persian army was definitively crushed in 642 at Nehavand (next to Hamadan). Persia fell under the domination of the Umayyad Caliphs, then the Abbassids.

The mosques built during this period were erected according to the so-called "Arab" mosque plan. The Arab mosque, probably influenced by the shape of the house in which Mohammed preached, includes a large courtyard surrounded by a hypostyle type prayer hall on one side and porticoes with columns on the other three sides, reminiscent of the Greek temenos. This layout is found in many Friday mosques, in particular in Damghan (1026), Fahraj (9th century), Nain (10th century) and Shushtar (9th century). The architectural elements that made up the fire temples of the Sassanian period influenced the shapes that the typical Iranian mosques used later.

These temples consisted of a courtyard, with a central altar covered with a cupola. In the same way, kiosk mosques are built in a square shape with an identical type of cupola. The mihrab was placed along the main axis indicating the direction of Mecca. One hall was added in the same axis, then, to hold more worshippers, a large courtyard was added to these constructions. During the Seljuk period, additional arched rooms were added around the courtyards in order to add an iwan on each side in the same axis. The typical Iranian mosque has four iwans. The most beautiful example is that of the Imam, on the Royal Square at Esfahan. The Iranian mosque's architecture has not changed for several centuries and has led to some beautiful mosques being built in many countries (Uzbekistan, Pakistan, India, even as far as China).

The walls were decorated in finely chiselled stucco between the 11th and 14th centuries. This was gradually replaced by mosaic, which made its first appearance around the 11th century and reached its peak under the reign of Shah Abbas I in the 16th and 17th centuries. During the Qadjar period, the colours changed considerably, with the introduction of pinks, yellows and greens. People and animals are represented in different forms and decorate various illustrations such as hunting scenes on official buildings and private houses.

House of Mohammed   Arab type mosque   Sassanian type   Persian type

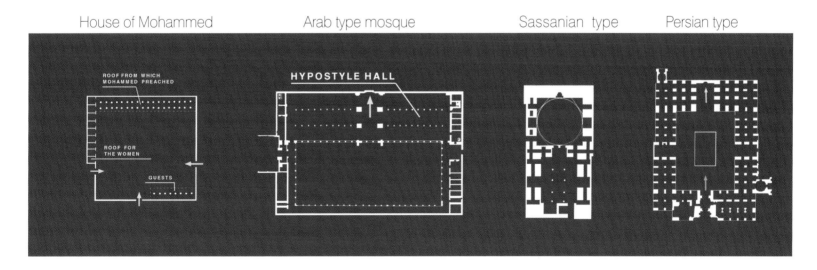

Islamic Iran

CITIES	MONUMENTS	800	900	1000	1100	1200	1300	1400	1500	1600	1700	1800	1900
Abarkuh	Friday Mosque							—					
Ardabil	Safi-al-Din mMausoleum							—					
Ardestan	Friday Mosque				—								
Bam	Citadel								—				
Bastam	Sheikh Bayazid Bastami Mausoleum						1296	1316					
	Minaret				1120								
Damghan	Minaret - Pir-e Alamdar funeral tower			1026									
Esfahan	All Saviour's cathedral									1606-1655			
	Tchehel Sotun									1647			
	Abbassi Hotel										1706-1714		
	Ismail Imamzadeh									1634			
	Jaffar Imamzadeh						1325						
	Madrasah-ye-Chahar Bagh										1706-1714		
	Haroun Velayat mausoleum								1513				
	Trembling minarets						1317						
	Ali Mosque and minaret					1135-1155			1521				
	Imam Mosque									1611			
	Sheikh Lotfollah Mosque								1598	1619			
	Friday Mosque			north and west iwans			1310	1447	—				
	Ali Qapu Palace							—	—				
	Hasht Behesht Palace									1699		1880	
	Royal Square									—			
	Pol-e Khadju									1650			
	Pol-e Djubi									1602			
	Pol Si-o-Seh (Tchechmeh Pol)									1600			
Fahraj	Friday Mosque	—											
Gonbad-e Qabus	Funeral tower			1006									
Gorgan	Friday Mosque - minaret				—								
	Nur Imamzadeh						—						
Kashan	Agha Bozorg Mosque and Madrasah									—			
	Borujerdi House											—	
	Tabatabei House											—	
	Bagh-e Fin									—			
	Abu Lolo Imamzadeh									—			
	Ibrahim Imamzadeh											—	
Kerman	Gombad-e Djabaliyeh												
	Friday Mosque						1348		—				
	Pa Menar Mosque						—						
	Imam Mosque			—									
	Caravanserai										—		

CITIES	MONUMENTS	800	900	1000	1100	1200	1300	1400	1500	1600	1700	1800	1900
Mahan	Bagh-e Tarikhi											▬	
	Shah Nematollah Vali Mausoleum						▬			▬		▬	
Mashhad	North iwan Shah Abbas II								▬	▬			
	South iwan Tala-ye Ali Shir Navâ'i							▬					
	Iman Reza Mausoleum									1675			
	Gohar Shad Mosque							1405-1447					
	Rabi Mausoleum									1617-1622			
Nain	Friday Mosque		▬										
Natanz	Abd-el-Samad funeral complex						1304-1309						
Qazvin	Ali Qapu Palace											▬	
	Imam Mosque										▬		
	Friday Mosque				▬				▬			▬	
	Hossein Imamzadeh								▬			▬	
	Haydariye Madrasah				▬								
Qom	Sanctuary										▬		
Semnan	Friday Mosque					▬		1425					
	Imam Khomeiny Mosque											▬	
Shiraz	Shah Cheragh Mausoleum					▬						▬	
	Sayyed Mir Mohammed Mausoleum											▬	
	Masdjed-e Atiq	▬					▬			▬			
	Nasir al Molk Mosque											▬	
	Ya Khan Madrasah									1615			
	Gavan mo-Mok											▬	
	Bagh-e Eram											▬	
	Arq Karim Khan										▬		
	e Vakil mosque										▬	▬	
Soltanieh	Sultan Uldjaïtu Mausoleum						1304-1347						
Susa	Tomb of Daniel					▬							
Tabriz	Blue Mosque							1436-1467					
Tehran	White Palace - Shah's summer residence												▬
	Golestan Qadjar Palace											▬	
	Imam Khomeiny Mosque											1830	
	Azadi -Tower - arch of liberty												1971
Yazd	Friday Mosque						1375						
	Tower of silence	▬											
	Dowlat Abad Garden House											▬	
	Mir Chakhmaq Mosque							1437					
	Vaqt-o-Sa'at Mosque						1325						
	Mausoleum of the twelve imams				▬								
Zavareh	Friday Mosque			1139									

Ardabil, on the route that leads from Tabriz to the Caspian Sea, is the hometown of Sheikh Safi al-Din (1252-1334), founder of the Shi'ite military brotherhood of the Quizzilbach and ancestor of Shah Ismail (1502-1524), the first sovereign of the prestigious Safavid dynasty.

The mausoleum is flanked by a tower of glazed bricks whose patterns were inspired by Timurid art.

nside, the sculpted wood sarcophagi of Sheikh Safi al-Din and his two sons are on show behind a silver grid.
The tomb of Shah Ismail, who was buried in 1524, was placed in a separate chamber. The whole building is sumptuously decorated with precious pieces from Khatam and wooden walls with carved ivory inscriptions.

nitially, the Friday mosque at Ardestan was of hypostyle type, and was enveloped by the newly built mosque in 1160. It is probably the oldest mosque with four iwans in Iran.

The fact that its minaret is not in the centre could imply that it was erected in the old central courtyard. In the hall with a cupola, the magnificent sculpted plaster covered mihrab was reworked in the 13th century under the Mongols.

The "Ark" citadel at Bam occupied a key position on the road to the east, which meant it was placed under siege several times. It was built by the Safavids and is enclosed in a double wall. We enter the town through a large monumental gate with a guardroom. It is a maze of small streets, a labyrinth destined to destabilise invaders. Today, all that remains are the desert and ruins, since Loft Ali Khan, the last of the Zends, took refuge there and was unable to resist the Qadjar Agha Mohammed, who put the population to the sword in 1794.

After the second wall, we climb up to the castle courtyard; this part has been well restored.

The small town of Bastam, 8 km from Sharud is visited by a large number of pilgrims who come to meditate at the tomb of the Sufi Sheikh Abou Yazid, who died in 874. He is better known by the name of Bayazid Bastami.

The current buildings date from 1313. The sarcophagus, placed under the cone-shaped roof in turquoise ceramic was made in the 18th century.

The adjacent mosque has an iwan decorated with stalactites and geometrical designs.

To the right of the mausoleum is the imamzadeh Mohammed Bastam Mirza (entrance iwan and cone-shaped funeral tower with blue mosaics).

DAMGHAN

The town of Damghan, at the foot of the southern slope of the Alborz on the road from Tehran to Mashhad, was invaded numerous times, by Arabs, Mongols and Timurids, and was destroyed by the Afghans in 1723.

Several Seljuk constructions remain: the tall minaret of the Friday mosque built in the 11th century, decorated with geometrical motifs (left), and the circular funeral tower (above) of Pir-e Alamdar also built in brick with Kufic inscriptions.

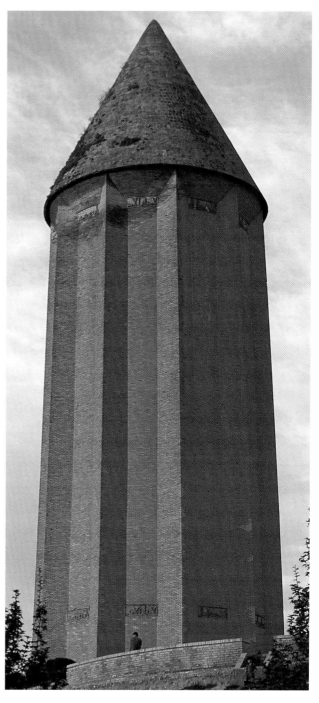

Fahraj

Gonbad-e Qabus

The mosque of Fahraj, 30 km to the east of Yazd, was built around the end of the 9th century; it is one of the oldest mosques in Iran. This is a hypostyle structure, its central courtyard surrounded by arcades with massive, undecorated pillars.

The halls are covered with small cupolas covered in ochre earth. One of the porticoes is a little deeper to show the direction of Mecca (qibla wall). The simply shaped minaret is the same earth colour as the walls.

The funeral tower of king Ziyarides Qabus (who died in 1012) can be seen from a distance, it is 54 m high and built on an artificial hillock so it looks even higher.

It is made of brick, and its proportions, shape and simple decoration make it unique in Iran. There are no stairs inside or outside up to the top, yet a glass coffin was apparently attached to the dome

GORGAN

Due to its location on the north slope of mount Alborz, on the borders of the Turkmenian steppes of Central Asia, Gorgan is on the edge of two worlds. On one side are the green fertile plains, which enjoy a temperate climate due to the mountains and the nearby Caspian Sea, and on the other side are the arid plains of the nomads.

Peoples have often come into conflict here, and the area has suffered a number of earthquakes.

The Friday mosque (above) has been restored several times. The interesting element is the brick minaret with its geometric drawings and inscriptions. Not far away in the bazaar is the Nur mausoleum (right), which dates from the 14th century and was built in the form of a brick tower.

The Tchehel Sotun, or pavilion with "forty columns", actually has only twenty, but the reflected image doubles their number. In the Orient, forty is a key figure (Ali Baba and the forty thieves, the forty days and forty nights of the flood, etc.).

The Tchehel Sotun was built under the reign of Shah Abbas I and extended by Shah Abbas II. It was used for official receptions and welcoming ambassadors. The portico, with its sumptuous ceiling decorated with marquetry, opens onto an iwan where the throne stood, facing the park, the ornamental pond and the fountains.
The water element and the reflections from the mirrors link the inside and outside.
The walls of the reception hall, which has been converted into a museum, are covered with historical compositions telling tales of battle.

The Khan-e Madar-e Shah caravanserai was built next to the madrasah of Shah Soltan Hossein's mother. The income from this establishment was used to provide for the teachers and pupils of the madrasah.

The premises became state property and were transformed into a luxury hotel to house important guests of the last shah. The hotel is now open to the public, enabling visitors to admire the central courtyard, the rooms and suites, and the reception and dining rooms.

The Jaffar Imamzadeh (opposite) is a small brick octagonal tower built in 1325, during the Mongol period. It was erected to protect the sepulchre of Jaffar, Mohammed's companion. This tomb supposedly also exists in other mausoleums. Each external side is decorated with a blind arch with a mosaic spandrel.

The Ismail Imamzadeh, finished in 1634 (below) was originally the tomb of the prophet Elie.
The complex includes a small "Chaïa" mosque and the courtyard of a madrasah. The decoration essentially consists of inscriptions.

This madrasah was commissioned by the mother of Shah Soltan Hossein and built between 1706 and 1714. It dates from the end of the Safavid dynasty and shows no signs of decay. The central courtyard was not designed like a mosque courtyard. It is a pleasant garden shaded by large plane trees and is crossed by a large marble canal that reflects the two principal east and west iwans.

It is surrounded by galleries with double arcades whose façades are decorated with mosaics, contrasting with the parge-work of the niches decorated with simple black and blue lines. There is a student's room in each alcove. The madrasah is still in activity; it is a school of theology.

The prayer room, which opens onto the courtyard through an iwan magnificently covered in mosaic, is covered by a dome whose tall drum includes a band covered in calligraphy. Two high minarets covered with decorations frame the building.

We know nothing about Haroun Velayat. Despite this, his mausoleum is highly venerated by the Esfahanis, especially by the women, who believe he has the power to cure sterility. The mausoleum was built under Shah Ismail I in 1513 and renovated under Shah Abbas II in 1656.
The enamelled ceramics at Esfahan are the most beautiful of this period.
The cenotaph stands in the middle of a room whose walls are covered with several styles of calligraphy.

The 50 m high Ali minaret (1131) can be seen from a great distance in the Esfahan countryside. It is the oldest of the town's 43 minarets. Its brick covering has various patterns: crosses and stars, and strips of writing.

The adjacent mosque dates from a later period (1521).

All that remains of a small 14th century Mongol mosque is an attractive iwan protecting the tomb of Sufi Sheikh Baba Abdallah.

The two minarets that frame this iwan are more recent; they were added in the 18th century. They have a specific feature that experts have been unable to explain: when you shake the top of one of the minarets, it oscillates and the second minaret oscillates with it.

The mosque of the Shah (Masdjed-e Shah) at the far south of the Royal Square is the first monument commissioned by Shah Abbas in 1612. It was only finished after his death in 1628, despite his impatience. To accelerate the building work, the tiles previously cut and baked separately were replaced by square painted tiles in various hues showing parts of the pattern (called "haft rangi" - seven colours).

This is the most grandiose of Iran's art monuments. Its proportions, and the harmony of its lines and colours, are remarkable. The ornamental pond in the central courtyard reflects the four iwans and the two-storey galleries that surround it. In front of the prayer room is an iwan flanked by two elegant minarets. The crowning cupola is covered in a mosaic, which resembles a tapestry, and a band with inscriptions covers the drum of its turquoise dome.

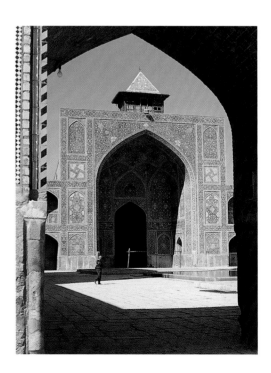

The entrance gate to the Sheikh Lotfollah mosque, set back from the Royal Square along its east side, is marked by a half-cupola archway decorated with enamelled stalactites.
There are no minarets, only a prayer room after a semi-dark L-shaped corridor. The prayer room is lit by a series of bay windows with grills cut into the drum supporting the cupola.

The decoration of the dome covered with blue and green arabesques, painted in black on a natural earth coloured background, is a marvel to behold.
Inside, on the walls and the cupola with a non-varnished beige background, are a series of blue and yellow drawings similar to the magnificent carpets that Iranian craftsmen are renowned for.

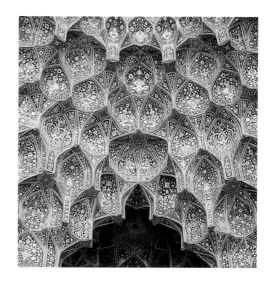

The Friday mosque (Masdjed-e Djomeh), the oldest in Esfahan, dates from three different periods:
-       the 11th century, under the Seljuks, built by the Shah Nizam al-Molk, the main prayer room and the south iwan (previous page and above);
-       the west iwan (next page) was reworked in 1700 by the Shah Soltan Hossein, because it is decorated with enamelled ceramic dating from the end of the Safavid period;
-       in the 14th century, the room containing the mihrab of the sultan Uldjaitu Khodabendeh, the grandson of Gengis Khan, and the winter room.

The south iwan seen from the terraces with its superb mosaics in enamelled ceramic
and its two minarets.

The north and west iwans (right), built during the Seljuk period, retain the primitive cell shape but the decoration was entirely carried out under the Safavids. The two minarets (above) that flank the south iwan are said to be the work of the chief Ouzoun Hassan (1453-1478) of the "white sheep" tribe, if we look at the inscription dated 1476.

The hall to the right of the west iwan was probably built under the Mozaffarids in the 14th century. It contains the famous mihrab (previous page) of the sultan Uldjaitu Khodabendeh (1310). The calligraphy and the floral patterns are in delicately sculpted stucco. To the right of the mihrab, the 17th century minbar is in marquetry. Next door, the winter room (1447) is squat and is free of decoration. The rooms around the courtyard have brick arches that are all different.

The Ali Qapu (high gate) palace stands in the middle of the Royal Square, on the west side, opposite the Lotfollah mosque. This imposing building, which remains elegant due to its slender first floor columns, was the gallery from which the Shah observed the various events that took place in the square (polo matches, military parades, etc.). It was also used for receptions for foreign dignitaries.

The columns and capitals on the first floor veranda or "Talar" are wooden, and the panelled ceilings are covered with marquetry.

The second floor, with its small salons, was reserved for banquets. The music room on the third floor is surrounded by niches on the walls and ceiling where pitchers and flasks were placed to improve the acoustics.

The Esfahan oasis owes its existence to the running water of the river Zayendeh Rud, which then disappears into the desert.

The Pol-e Khaju dam bridge, the most famous, 130 m long, has twenty-four arches and two levels of galleries with arcades.

It was built during the reign of Shah Abbas II in the middle of the 12th century to replace a Seljuk construction that was no longer sufficient.

Each arch was fitted with a vane allowing the water flow to be regulated and to control irrigation of the gardens downstream. The inhabitants of Esfahan come here for walks and to enjoy the coolness during hot summer days.

Shah Abbas I was a great urbanist. The work he had done on Royal Square is a masterful example of his talents. 500 m long and 150 m wide, the square is bordered with two-storey galleries that link up four major monuments of Esfahan. The monumental gate of the Shah, opposite the gate of the bazaar, is along the longitudinal axis. The Ali Qapu palace and the Lotfollah mosque lie along the other axis. Many types of shops are set up in the arcades round the edge. The current layout of the square no longer allows us to imagine what this vast esplanade must have been like when celebrations, polo matches and public executions took place.

The palace of Hasht Behesht ("eight paradises", above) is located in the niche of greenery in the Bagh-e Bolbol ("nightingale garden") park. This small palace, built under the Shah Soleiman (1669), was reworked by Fath Ali Shah (Qadjar). Its main hall, covered with a cupola, is surrounded by eight small salons.

The inhabitants of Esfahan like to walk along the banks of the river Zayendeh Rud and enjoy the views from the different bridges. There is Sio-Seh Pol, "the bridge with thirty-three arches" (below left), which was commissioned by Shah Abbas I to link the Armenian quarter to the centre of Esfahan (295 m long with two levels of arcades). A "chaikhaneh" was installed in the lower part. The Pol-e Djubi bridge (below right) takes its name from the canal it used to support.

K A S H A N

The Abu Lolo imamzadeh (opposite) is located to the left of the road that leads from Kashan to Bagh-e Fin. It is characterised by the cone-shaped roof of its main hall. The roof is decorated in turquoise and yellow ceramic.

On the other side of the same road is the charming Ibrahim imamzadeh (below), that was built during the Qadjar period.
A small peristyle with walls covered in mirrors is reflected in an ornamental pond surrounded by large trees. Two minarets frame the façade of the cenotaph room covered with a cone-shaped roof decorated with predominantly turquoise ceramic tiles.

We reach the Agha Bozorg mosque through the madrasah surrounded by a split-level courtyard. In the lower part, the galleries open onto a pleasant garden planted with trees and adorned with an ornamental pond. The main part of the madrasah is flanked by two wind towers that air the lower levels of the building. The mosque has two iwans. The iwan facing north towards the madrasah has two minarets, and leads to the mihrab room, which is covered with a plain brick cupola. The overall decoration is simple; the dominant ochre colour of the brick is brought out with a few ceramic patterns.

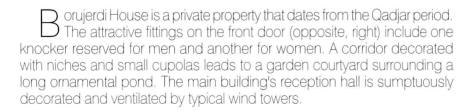

B orujerdi House is a private property that dates from the Qadjar period. The attractive fittings on the front door (opposite, right) include one knocker reserved for men and another for women. A corridor decorated with niches and small cupolas leads to a garden courtyard surrounding a long ornamental pond. The main building's reception hall is sumptuously decorated and ventilated by typical wind towers.

The front door of Tabatabei House (from the Qadjar period) has the same type of knockers as those of Borujerdi House. The interior is organised around the ornamental pond of the garden-courtyard. There is a two-level peristyle before the reception room, whose volume is considerably increased by the ornamental glass that decorates the walls.
The ornate façades have a succession of colonnades and niches.

The water that is so rare on the Iranian Plateau flows here in abundance from the nearby mountains.
Shah Abbas I, who noticed this cool spot, had a small palace built at Bagh-e Fin. It is richly decorated and laid out with gardens and a succession of canals and pools built in marble that flow into one another, providing a constant sound of waterfalls. The current pavilions date from the beginning of the 19th century.

Gonbad-e Djabaliyeh (opposite right) stands alone at the foot of the mountains to the east of Kerman. Its origin is unknown, but the Zoroastrians may have used it.

The dome rests on a double, octagonal drum. Unlike most buildings in the region, it was built in stone rather than brick.

The Pa Menar mosque (opposite left and below) has beautiful mosaics on its entrance gate that was built in 1300 under the Timurids.

The Friday mosque, built in 1348 under the Mozaffarids (a local dynasty), was considerably restored in the 16th century by the Safavids. Its rectangular plan with four iwans corresponds to the Iranian mosque shape. An extremely attractive entrance pishtag with a half-cupola on a squinch is reflected in a large pool, which brings out its true beauty.

Its wealth of decoration in enamelled ceramic plays on a varied range of cobalt blue, turquoise and tropical blue as well as shades of yellow.

It is extremely interesting to walk through the Vakil Bazaar (Regent's Bazaar) due to the succession of varied public buildings found on both sides of the main alley. These include mosques, hammams, caravanserais and madrasahs. This caravanserai (above and below) has kept magnificent wind towers, ornate cupolas and has small domes that jut out on the veranda that runs along its entire length.

These valuable buildings generally date from the Safavid period and are often badly maintained or abandoned. At the far end of this square (above and below), the madrasah under restoration is being used by architects who are surveying it. These areas are always very lively, and the crowds from the bazaar come to relax here.

97

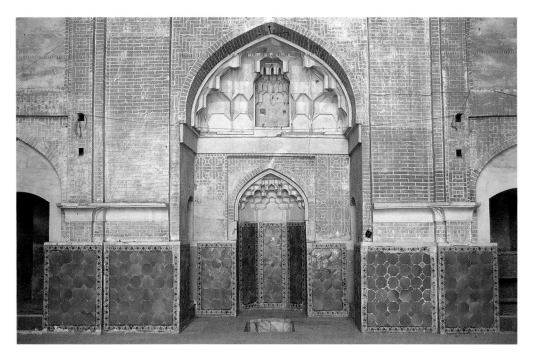

The e-Malek mosque at Kerman (now known as the Imam mosque) has been restored a number of times.
It originally dates from the 11th century, the Seljuk period - several elements from this era are still visible: the dome and some inscriptions.
Work is currently being carried out, bringing to light three small mihrabs (opposite right) in sculpted stucco on the terrace next to the cupola.

The small town of Mahan is surrounded by the desert, and the mountains behind it rise to almost 4,000 metres.

Close by, a patch of green looks like a true oasis. The water that made it possible to build this delicious garden, shaded by large trees, flows abundantly.

In the central axis, a series of pools, channels, waterfalls and fountains uses the slope of the land to keep the water in constant movement.

Two pavilions punctuate the lower part of the entrance (opposite) and the starting point for the water show in the top part (below).

The mausoleum that houses the remains of Nour-ed Din-Nematollah Vali, founder of an order of dervishes, was built in 1431 by a Muslim king from India. It was extended and restored during the reign of Shah Abbas I, and was restored again under the Qadjars.

The central square hall is covered with a dome decorated in blue ceramic and white interlacings (the work of Shah Abbas). Two rooms with barrel arches are juxtaposed and open onto the room containing the dervish's tomb.

A monumental gate flanked by two minarets opens onto the courtyard, which was built under the Qadjars.

Mashhad, the holy city of Shi'ite Islam is an important destination for pilgrims with its sanctuary built in memory of Ali Reza, the eighth Imam, who was buried in 817. Since then, his tomb and the city itself have been destroyed and rebuilt several times. A few buildings are grouped around the mausoleum (the Gohar Shad mosque, three madrasahs and a museum) forming a complex known as the "sanctuary" (haram). In principle, non-Muslims may only access the courtyards and the museum.

In the view of the haram (above), we can see the extraordinary road system being built to handle the considerable flow of pilgrims. Starting from the left, we can see the dome and the south iwan flanked by two minarets of the Gohar Shad mosque built in 1405 under the Timurids, then the Imam Reza mausoleum, erected in the 12th century, rebuilt and restored a number of times, and whose dome and golden minarets date from 1675.

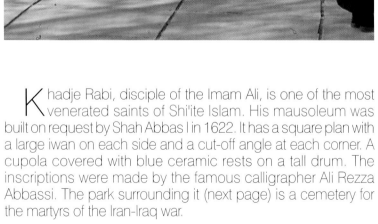

Khadje Rabi, disciple of the Imam Ali, is one of the most venerated saints of Shi'ite Islam. His mausoleum was built on request by Shah Abbas I in 1622. It has a square plan with a large iwan on each side and a cut-off angle at each corner. A cupola covered with blue ceramic rests on a tall drum. The inscriptions were made by the famous calligrapher Ali Rezza Abbassi. The park surrounding it (next page) is a cemetery for the martyrs of the Iran-Iraq war.

NAIN

The entrance gate and minaret of the Friday mosque, on the square of the small town of Nain, stand out. The mosque is from the Abbassid period and dates from around 960. It is of the so-called "Arab" hypostyle type, and the courtyard is square and has no iwans. The inside pillars are massive and the porticoes narrow, but the sculpted plaster decoration, especially that of the mihrab, is remarkable. The 14th century minbar is entirely made of sculpted wood.

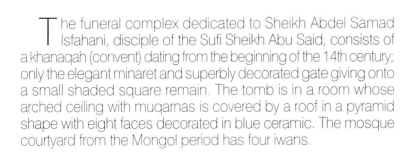

The funeral complex dedicated to Sheikh Abdel Samad Isfahani, disciple of the Sufi Sheikh Abu Said, consists of a khanaqah (convent) dating from the beginning of the 14th century; only the elegant minaret and superbly decorated gate giving onto a small shaded square remain. The tomb is in a room whose arched ceiling with muqarnas is covered by a roof in a pyramid shape with eight faces decorated in blue ceramic. The mosque courtyard from the Mongol period has four iwans.

The Safavids established their capital at Qazvin and then
transferred it to Esfahan in 1598 under the reign of Shah
Abbas I. A small pavilion remains from this era, the Tchehel Sotun,
located in the centre of the town in a pretty park. This residence
has two storeys, and the first floor has a gallery running round it
with wooden beams. It is a foretaste of the types of residences
later found in Esfahan.

The Shahzadeh Hossein mausoleum (above) is set in the middle of a courtyard whose entrance is characteristic of the Qadjar period, topped with small minarets.
A peristyle, whose walls and ceiling stalactites are entirely covered with mirrors, is before the room where the cenotaph rests. It is decorated with marquetry from the Safavid era.

The remaining point of interest is the kiosk with cupola of the Haydariye madrasah (a reminder of the Sassanian fire temples), which was formerly a mosque. Its decoration is 12th century Seljuk, and we can admire the sculpted plaster arabesques of the mihrab (opposite), the drawings of fruit and the Kufic inscriptions.

The Imam mosque is quite recent (it probably dates from the beginning of the 19th century); its ceramics are similar to those found in Shiraz.

There are no longer any remains of the earliest part of the Friday mosque, which dated from the beginning of the Islamic period.

It was rebuilt by Khurmartash, a vassal of the Seljuk sovereign Malek Shah (1072-1092), and the mihrab room remains from this period. Later restoration work was performed with the addition of the iwans and galleries under Shah Abbas II.

The south iwan (opposite) is covered in enamelled ceramic in the same style as the Esfahan monuments.

The prayer room is covered with a large Seljuk dome decorated with Kufic characters.

Qom is the second holy city of Iran after Mashhad. It has a sanctuary devoted to Fatima, the sister of the Imam Reza, who died in 816.

The sanctuary, inaccessible to non-Muslims is dominated by several domes and minarets covered in enamelled ceramic tiles.

The dome of the Fatima sanctuary is recognisable because it is covered in gold. It was rebuilt under Shah Abbas I after suffering considerable damage under the Mongols and Tamerlane.

SEMNAN

The mosque of the Imam Khomeiny (formerly the mosque of the Shah or the Royal mosque) was erected at the beginning of the 19th century under the Qadjar Dath Ali Shah. Its enamelled ceramic with flowers and arabesques are characteristic of the period.

The minaret of the Friday mosque, separate from the rest of the buildings, dominates the town of Semnan. It was built during the Seljuk era (11th or 12th century) entirely of brick with geometric patterns.

The large iwan that leads to the prayer room, the only iwan here, dates from the Timurid period in the 15th century. Inside, the mihrab is surrounded by sculpted plaster.

The mausoleum of Amir Ahmad, brother of the Imam Reza, known as Shah Cheragh "the king of the lamp", who died in 835, is one of the major pilgrimage sites for Shi'ite Muslims. It was built in the 13th century and has been restored several times. Its dome collapsed during an earthquake and was rebuilt in the 19th century in its characteristic bulb shape.

The floral patterns of the ceramic tiles are in muted cream and turquoise shades.

In the same courtyard, close to the Shah Cheragh mausoleum, stands the Sayyed Mir Mohammed mausoleum. It was built in the 19th century, during the Qadjar period. Sayyed Mir Mohammed was also a brother of the Imam Reza.

The cenotaph room is also covered with a pear-shaped dome.

After the Mir Mohammed mosque, you walk under a porch (opposite) to reach Masdjed-e Atiq, the Friday mosque or ancient mosque, founded in 875. It was the work of Amr-Ebn-e Leid of the Safavid dynasty. It was rebuilt in the 12th century and restored in the 17th century.

In the courtyard stands the house of the Koran, the "bayt al-Mushaf", erected in 1351. Its plan is square and it is flanked by a tower on each corner.
This small building was designed to house holy books such as the Koran.

The entrance gate of the Nasir al Molk mosque (above), which stands in a small side street, does not even hint at the beauty of the building hidden away behind the walls.

Two iwans frame the central courtyard to the north and south, and there are two prayer rooms on the longer sides.

The coloured mosaics of the south iwan (previous page) are reflected in a rectangular pool.

With its façades and part of the interior covered with ceramic mosaics, this mosque is one of the most beautiful examples from the Qadjar period in the late 19th century.

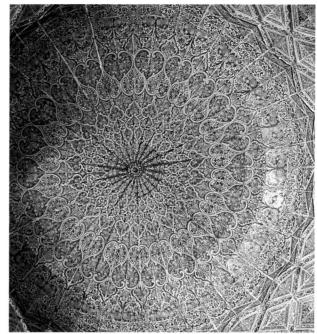

The prayer room on the western side of the courtyard (previous page, above and below right) is splendid. The mosaics covering the walls, arches and small cupolas, completed with stained glass, give a delightful harmony of colours.
The decoration of the other prayer room (below left), symmetrical across the courtyard, is less ornate.

123

The richness and variety of patterns - arabesques, flowers, vases, landscapes, etc. - make this complex remarkable.

With the appearance of pink shades, the range of colours was richer during the Qadjar period. The greens, yellows and blues are of different shades to those used in previous centuries.

The Imam Qouli Khan, governor of the Fars region during the reign of Shah Abbas, had several buildings erected that enhance the city of Shiraz, in particular the Ya Khan madrasah, built in 1615.

The interior courtyard is surrounded by galleries with double arcades that lead to the theology students' rooms.

The mosaics are more recent and date from the school of Qadjar painters and mosaicists at the beginning of the 19th century.

Various flowers - roses, pink carnations and violet irises - surrounded by many branches with wide green leaves and birds were sources of inspiration at Shiraz, known as the "rose garden".

126

After crossing the deserts of the Fars, travellers appreciate the gardens of Shiraz, which used to surround the city with a green belt.

A few public gardens, such as the "Bagh-e Eram" are still in existence, and give a glimpse of the charm of the city. The Eram garden, with its central pavilion built by the Qadjar governor Mohammed Ghli Khan-e-Ilkhani, has its "Bonegah", the forerunner of the Sassanian gardens.

This is the private part of the park with its circular fence planted with plane trees, poplars and flowers. The "Sarv-e Naz" is found there; this is the emblematic tree of the people of Shiraz: a tall, slender cypress.

G avan Mo-Mok was the private residence of a notable of Shiraz under the Qadjars. There are two pavilions facing one another across a rectangular pool surrounded by majestic trees and flowerbeds.

The iwan of the main pavilion leads to several rooms, on the ground floor and the first floor, which are richly decorated with painted wood and marquetry. The walls covered with mirrors enhance the natural decoration by extending the perspective of the gardens towards the interior.

The subjects of these Qadjar mosaics are many and new - lions, soldiers and horsemen, and portraits of concubines on the ceilings.

The imposing 18th century fortress called Qalaeh-ye-Karim Khan is the work of the regent Karim Khan Zend. This square building is surrounded on all four sides by high thick walls reinforced at the corners by cylindrical bastions.
The complex was built of bricks that make decorative patterns on the towers.
Inside, Karim Khan had his room, his guards and his administration. Municipal offices now occupy the premises.

The Masdjed-e Vakil, the "mosque of the Regent" is another 18th century building erected during the reign of Karim Kahn Zend (a sovereign who did not wish to be called King). The main gate (above) was restored in the 19th century and is decorated with floral motifs. Two iwans frame the courtyard. The south iwan leads to the prayer room, which is in the same style as that of the Nasir al Molk mosque, with small cupolas supported by rows of columns.

SOLTANIEH

In the 14th century, Soltanieh "the Imperial" was a Mongol capital whose apogee was under the sultan Uljaitu Khodabendeh (1304-1316). The sultan converted to Shi'ite Islam, and had this mausoleum built in 1306 to receive the remains of the martyr Imams Ali and Hossein. This was rejected, so he decided to keep this funeral mosque for himself. It was built in brick, in an octagonal shape, and is covered with a superb curved, ribbed cupola placed on four squinches, decorated at each corner with a small minaret (now cut off). Inside, it is decorated with multi-coloured ceramics and sculpted plaster.

The blue mosque of Tabriz, built under the reign of Djahan Shah (sovereign of the Black Sheep tribe, 1436-1467), is a good example of Timurid art. It is renowned for its splendid mosaics, comparable to those of Samarkand, which can be seen on the gate (above). The shades are varied - the famous turquoise and dark blue of Tabriz, red-brown, yellow ochre, golden yellow, green and black. The flowers and inscriptions are enveloped in interlacings and arabesques.

The ruins of Susa, a city that flourished from the fourth millennium BC to the 11th century of the Christian era, appear as a series of mounds that are the remains of archaeological digs. Nothing of interest remains at the site, or in the museum.

In the village, a white cupola in the shape of a sugar loaf tops the mausoleum of the prophet Daniel, who is highly venerated by Muslims. Historians indicate that it existed as early as the 14th century, but the façade with its iwan and its small minarets is relatively recent. The cenotaph room is covered with mirrors.

TEHRAN

Like a monumental gate to the west of Tehran, at the intersection of the roads from the airport and Qazvin, stands the Azadi tower, the "arch of liberty". It was built in 1971 to celebrate 2,500 years of the monarchy. It was originally called the Shahyade, "Souvenir of the Shah".
It is entirely built from white stone from the surrounding areas, and, at 45 m high, dominates the city. A cultural centre, a museum, exhibition galleries and a library have been installed in its upper floors.
The Azadi tower is not only a cultural centre, but is also a place where the city's inhabitants go to walk and to relax.

The eighteen Pahlavi residences dating from 1930 were built in very attractive grounds of 120 hectares, called "Sa'ad Abad" on the high ground to the north of Tehran. The Shah's summer residence, known as the "white palace", where he only lived for three months a year, is an austere building with a two-storey colonnade topped with an imposing cornice. There are some magnificent objects in the rooms: dishes from France and Germany, Sèvres china, extremely valuable carpets, antique furniture, etc. The large pair of bronze boots close to the steps (opposite) are from a statue of the Shah that was destroyed during the revolution.

The Golestan, which means "palace of the roses", which was begun by Aqa Mohammed Qadjar and finished by Fath Ali Shah at the beginning of the 19th century, consists of several buildings around a park with pools, rose beds and huge plane trees.

The palace, which was used as a residence for the Qadjar kings, opens onto the gardens through a hall covered in ceramic tiles and mirrors, and houses the Peacock Throne that was used for official ceremonies. An iwan outside the palace protects a second throne (opposite). Everything is sculpted in marble and alabaster. This throne of Solomon surrounded by chimeras is called "Takht-e Marmar".

At the other end of the park, a building with several floors was set aside for the apartments of concubines. The ground floor was accessed via an imposing staircase, which gave onto a wide hall entirely decorated with mirrors and ceramic tiles. During the Qadjar period, the subjects used for decoration became more varied, and representations of human figures were widely used. Here we can see soldiers and hunters as well as landscapes.

141

Each concubine's apartment has a deep loggia with a view of the gardens.
The marble bas-reliefs of the platform base represent the soldiers of the guard. They appear to be posted all along the building to ensure the concubines' safety.

The mosque known as the "Imam Khomeiny" mosque (previously the mosque of the Shah) is attached to the bazaar and even has a door that communicates directly with it. It was built at the request of Fath Ali in 1809, and remains one of Tehran's principal monuments. The square courtyard with four iwans is surrounded by galleries with arcades following the Iranian mosque design.

The south iwan leads to the prayer room, topped with a dome decorated with blue and white chevrons and covered with a highly curved golden dome.

The enamelled ceramics decorated with arabesques and flowers on a yellow background date from the Qadjar period.

143

The panorama from the terraces of the houses of Yazd includes a large number of wind towers and the Friday mosque, which is recognisable due to its high pishtag (previous page), its two slender minarets, and its ochre dome broken up by black and blue diamond shapes.

It was built in the 14th century and has just one iwan on a courtyard, which leads to the prayer room whose mihrab (1375) is a masterpiece with stalactites in enamelled ceramic.

The Mir Chakhmaq mosque is accessed from the grand bazaar square via a narrow porch that opens onto a square courtyard surrounded by one floor of galleries and four iwans. The prayer room is covered with a dome decorated with blue and ochre mosaics. Its mihrab is entirely in sculpted marble surrounded by turquoise, enamelled ceramic tiles.

It bears the name of the governor of Yazd who had it built in 1436 during the Timurid period.

The "Dowlat Abad Garden" house dates from 1787. It stands in the middle of a green oasis, which accentuates the ochre shade of its walls. The large wind tower, which ensures ventilation, rises up among the cypress and pine trees. The octagonal reception room located in the centre communicates on two levels with several small rooms set in the cut-off angles, and some on the first floor that lead to balconies.

An ingenious system, due to the height of the tower, ensures efficient ventilation, and enables drafts to be created during the cool hours of the day.

The pishtag (opposite) of the mosque of the Time and Hour, "Vaqt-o-Sa'at", is recent and does not reflect the architecture of the buildings, built by Said Rokn ed Din in 1326, which are no longer in existence.
These included a madrasah, a library and an observatory.

After walking through a maze of streets, we come to the "Mausoleum of the Twelve Imams" (below). It dates from the Seljuk period (11th century) and is entirely built in brick and covered with a brick dome.
Inside, in the prayer room, there is an attractive, well-preserved sculpted plaster mihrab.

SHUSHTAR

I n Shushtar, in the centre of the old town, the Friday mosque is recognisable due to its minaret, which is characteristic of the Mongol period (late 13th century). It is entirely built of bricks, some of which are coloured and varnished.

The prayer room of Abbassid type (866) is one of the oldest in Iran, with its massive pillars. The mihrab and the minbar date from the 12th century.

153

AZERBAİJAN

TURKMENISTAN

TURKEY

Maku

Ghara
Kelisa

Jolfa
Kelisa
Qarre Sham

Tabriz

Orumieh lake

Ardabil

CASPIAN SEA

Gorgan

Gonbad-e Qavus

MAZANDARAN

KHORASSAN

Mashhad

Soltanieh

Alumut

Bastam

Qazvin

ALBORZ

Damghan

Tehran

Semnan

Hamadan

Dasht-e Kevir

Qom

Kashan

Natanz

Zavareh

Ardestan

AFGHANISTAN

LORESTAN

Nain

KHUZISTAN

Susa

Esfahan

Yazd

IRAQ

Shuhstar

Rud-e Karun

ZAGROS

Faraj

KERMAN

Abarkuh

Dasht-e Lut

Kerman

Mahan

Shiraz

Bam

PAKISTAN

Kuwait

SAUDI ARABIA

PERSIAN GULF

GULF OF OMAN

from -40 to 500 meters
from 500 to 1000 meters
from 1000 to 1500 meters
from 1500 to 2000 meters
from 2500 to 3000 meters
from 3000 to 4000 meters
over 4000 meters

● Town
● Christian site
- - - Present boundaries

0 km   100   200   300

CHRISTIANITY
IN IRAN

Under the Sassanians, all religions other than the state religion, Zoroastrianism, were severely repressed. This is why Armenians who had converted to Christianity were often accused of being allied with the Romans.

In Tabriz and the area around it, there is still an Armenian community of almost 190,000 believers. Every year, in July, they go on a pilgrimage to Saint Thaddeus church ("Ghara Kelisa") to commemorate the anniversary of the death of Saint Thaddeus who came to the region to evangelise it and create a sanctuary. He was martyred and is buried in his church.

At the border with Azerbaijan, the small town of Jolfa used to be highly prosperous and was inhabited by Armenian Christians.

In 1603, Shah Abbas I deported a large number of Armenian families from the town and established them in the district of Jolfa in Esfahan in order to encourage trade. He gave them a number of privileges, which included their own administration with a mayor and complete religious freedom with the right to build churches. The district flourished with beautiful residences and places of worship, such as the All Saviours' cathedral and the Bethlehem church. The sovereigns who followed Shah Abbas did not maintain these privileges, and the community, which had grown to almost 60,000, was persecuted in the centuries that followed. However, the district still stands and retains a Christian way of life with churches where worship still takes place today.

ESFAHAN

Shah Abbas the Great set up Armenian families in a suburb of Esfahan called Jolfa. His aim was to prevent them from falling into the hands of the Turks and to take advantage of their skills as tradesmen, excellent masons and architects. He allowed them privileges and authorised them to build churches.

All Saviours' cathedral, which was built in 1606 and extended in 1655, does not look like a church from the outside, because its façades and cupola have been covered with bricks to prevent it from collapsing. The inside is completely different: it looks like a Christian place of worship with frescoes on the walls. The paintings are of European influence, both Italian and Dutch. There is a Last Judgement, and scenes of the suffering and martyrdom of Saint Gregory.

The apostle Saint Thaddeus (Jude, brother of James) came to evangelise the region in 66 AD and had the first sanctuary built. He was martyred and buried in his own church.

In a splendid mountain landscape, close to Mount Ararat and the Turkish border, the basilica stands out against its austere surroundings.

It was built in the shape of a cross and consists of a chevet in black and pale stone covered with a cupola, which dates from the 11th century. The centre of the basilica is built of light-coloured sandstone, topped with a tall drum with twelve facets, each with an opening. A cupola crowns the whole building.

It was significantly restructured in the 19th century, and has just been very well restored.

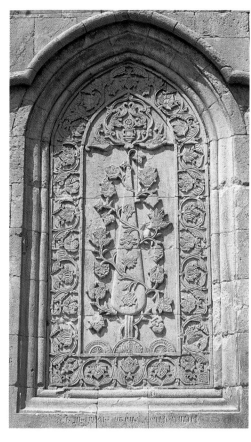
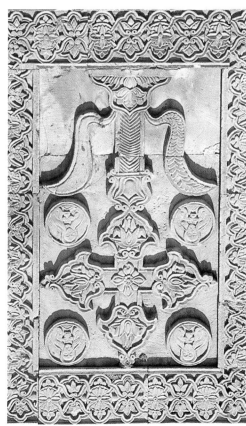

159

The interior decoration is very plain, with no sculptures or frescoes. The façades, however, are covered with bas-reliefs in the form of panels representing different motifs - various crosses, effigies of saints, animals in varying positions, etc. A series of vine leaves alternated with animals form a frieze which runs round the walls.

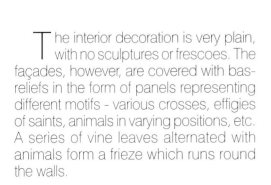

S aint Stephen's church, the Kelisa Darre Sham, huddled in the crook of the mountain in the free zone between Iran and Azerbaijan, close to Jolfa, dominates the Rud-e Aras valley. The Armenian families sent to Esfahan at the beginning of the 17th century by Shah Abbas the Great came from this region. This church, built in the 14th century, was rebuilt and fortified in the 16th century. The main building, which forms the centre of the cross, is covered with a cupola raised up by a drum with twelve panels with six openings only (one every other panel). The choir is covered by a smaller cupola.

The façade is decorated with bas-reliefs that have been directly carved into the stones.
The crosses carved into the red-ochre sandstone follow one another, and all have a different design.
The pediment of the square and the panels of the drum (above) are richly decorated with sculptures.

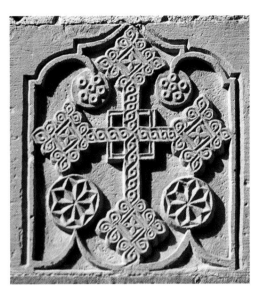

The entrance door to the church (previous page) is small for a building of this size.
The choir and its chevet (above).
The cupola of the transept and its drum pierced with openings (opposite).

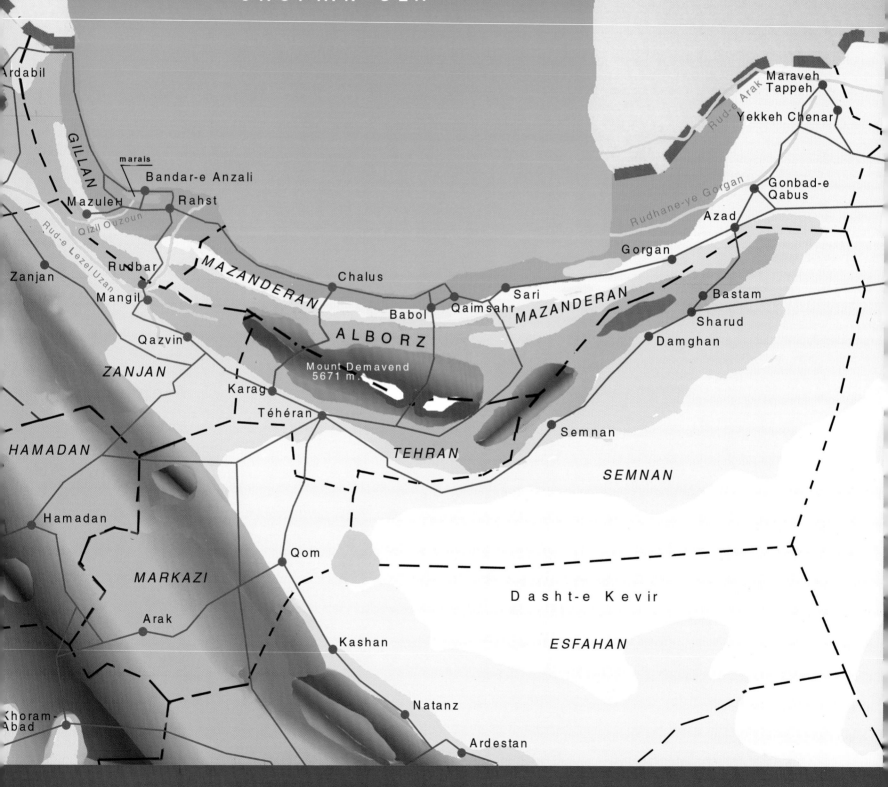

THE NORTH

Provinces

of

TEHRAN
GILAN
and
MAZANDERAN

The province of **Tehran**, the smallest in Iran, with a high population density (20% of the country's population), extends south of the Alborz mountain chain to the outskirts of the Dasht-e Kevir desert. The province's economy was initially agriculture-based, and Tehran has developed into the largest industrial centre in the country over the last thirty years.

The climate varies according to altitude. The areas bordering on the desert are hot and dry in summer, but the temperatures are pleasant in the nearby mountains, where you can walk, climb (Demavend peaks at 5,671 m) and ski in winter.

Archaeological investigations revealed a 3,000-year-old cemetery at Tepe-Gayatarieh (Chemiran). It was also a meeting place for long caravans, but for centuries, the region played a secondary role only.

It was not until the 18th century that the Qadjars showed an interest in the site and established their capital city there (1789). They had several royal palaces built: Sahebqaranieh to the north of the city, the Golestan to the south, and the mosque of the Shah, now called the Imam Khomeiny mosque.

Gilan and **Mazanderan** provinces stretch from the border of the newly independent state of Azerbaijan to Turkmenistan, between the Caspian Sea and the Alborz mountains. The mountains cut off these provinces from the rest of the country, and the climate is very different - hot and humid. Clouds coming in from over the Caspian Sea remain cloaked over the north slopes. The vegetation is luxuriant close to the sea and on the flanks of the mountains.

In **Gilan** province, the population is concentrated along the coast, around Rasht, and in the valley of the Sefi Rud River. The province was isolated for a long time, and has kept its traditions - dialect, craftsmanship (carpet weaving) and its typical style of dwellings (large wooden houses with thatched roofs).

Tea cultivation, the principal wealth of the region, was introduced at the beginning of the 20th century by an Iranian diplomat posted to India.

The plain widens in **Mazanderan** province stretching towards the steppes of Central Asia in the east. These lands have often been invaded through the centuries. Most of the inhabitants are Turkmen who have become settled, but who have retained their traditional customs, costumes and language.

TEHRAN

The city of Tehran, Iran's capital, extends across the slopes of the foothills of the Alborz Mountains (whose highest peak, Mount Demavend, rises to 5,671 m), then slopes gently down towards the desert. The city stretches more than 30 km from north to south and from east to west, and its altitude varies from 1,700 m to 1,100 m.

Tehran's population is constantly increasing, growing more than seventeen-fold in fifty years; there are now over ten million inhabitants. Tehran was probably founded in the 11th century, and was chosen as the capital in 1789 under the Qadjars, replacing Shiraz. There are few monuments: the Azadi tower, the Golestan, and the palaces in the Sa'ad Abad park (next page and seen previously).

170

171

The city is criss-crossed in places on both sides of the streets with open canals flanked by tall plane trees (above). Water sometimes flows in abundance, even creating waterfalls due to the slope of the land. These canals are the "djub", which were formerly used to supply water to all districts of the city. No panorama is visible from the avenues running from east to west, but those running northwards open onto the snow-covered Alborz Mountains (below).

The bazaar is a hive of feverish activity during the run-up to the anniversary of the death of Hussein (next page).

The Alborz Mountains form a solid wall facing the coast of the Caspian Sea. They can only be crossed in a few places, and with difficulty.

From the border with Azerbaijan (opposite and bottom left next page) to that of Turkmenistan (former Soviet republic), the north face of the mountains has a temperate and humid climate, which encourages the growth of luxuriant vegetation. The temperature and humidity of this region make it possible to grow rice, tea, and various citrus fruits (above and top of the next page).

MAZULEH

The road that runs along the Caspian coast is of little interest, as there are simply a succession of heteroclite and anarchic constructions. You need to climb the small valleys perpendicular to the mountains to find dwellings and a lifestyle that retain their traditional charm.

If you climb up the Qizil Ouzoun valley, you reach Mazuleh, one of the most beautiful villages in Gilan province. Its houses with wooden balconies and verandas nestle on the flanks of the mountains.

فیلم عکاسی
موجودات
۱۱۰ ۱۳۰ ۱۲۵

The dwellings of Gilan province, between the banks of the Caspian Sea and the mountains, are unique in Iran. The materials used are generally wood for the structures, floors and galleries, and thatch for the roofs. The roofs are usually sharply sloped with overhangs, because of the frequent and heavy rainfall in the region. The peasants still dress simply in white shirts and black trousers with a typical small skullcap.

Due to the constant humidity, the buildings are always on raised foundations. On ground level are stables and sheds, and all or part of the living quarters are on the first floor.

BANDAR-E ANZALI

Bandar-e Anzali was a Russian trading post for fishing concessions in the 19th century, and has remained Iran's main port on the Caspian Sea.

Sturgeon fishing in the river mouths and caviar production, mainly for export, remain significant sources of income. This business has become a state monopoly.

The marshes surrounding Anzali (below) have been drained, and are a haven for migratory birds.

The main road from Tehran to Mashhad first stretches for a long way between the Alborz Mountains and the Caspian Sea, then between the mountains and the vast plains of the land of the Turkmen.

The inhabitants of this region, in particular those living in Gorgan, have proudly kept their traditions and often their costumes.

On the 13th day of the new year (No Ruz, the Iranian new year), from the 1st to the 4th of Favardin (March 21st-24th), the tradition is that each family should leave their home (top of the next page) to picnic in the countryside on the banks of a river or stream and throw pebbles into the water. It is a sort of joyful exodus.

Like Gorgan, the town of Gonbad-e Qabus long suffered from the terrible Mongol invasions in the 13th century, followed by those of Tamerlane at the end of the 14th century and those of his descendants.

We are in Central Asia here, with Samarkand close by. The current population is Turkmen, which can be seen in the streets and the public parks. The men with slanted eyes and high cheekbones wear Astrakhan toques, and the women do not wear the chador, but flower-patterned dresses and brightly coloured headscarves. The most commonly used language in the streets and in the shops is Turkmen.

GORGAN

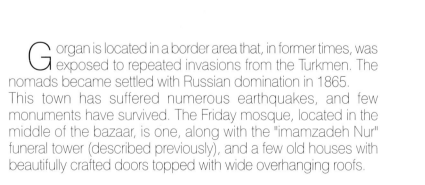

G organ is located in a border area that, in former times, was exposed to repeated invasions from the Turkmen. The nomads became settled with Russian domination in 1865. This town has suffered numerous earthquakes, and few monuments have survived. The Friday mosque, located in the middle of the bazaar, is one, along with the "imamzadeh Nur" funeral tower (described previously), and a few old houses with beautifully crafted doors topped with wide overhanging roofs.

I n this region, well off the main traffic routes, the landscapes remain intact and are superb.
The land is still worked manually, by men who repeat the timeless gestures of sowing by hand, even if the fertiliser they use today is probably a chemical one.

The Rudhane-ye Gorgan River, which brings water to the town of Gonbad-e Qabus, traces its path northwards. The small road that follows its course leads to Maraveh Tappeh. From there, there is no passage through to Turkmenistan, where the steppes of Central Asia begin.

In the Middle Ages, it was a communication route that enabled the invasions of all the peoples who came from the north, and one of the most frequented routes on the Silk Road, which led straight to Bukhara. Set in a landscape of green rolling hills, and the meandering course of a small river, we come across one of the many marvellous caravanserais.

After leaving the Rudhane-ye Gorgan River, climbing over a few peaks, and reaching the Rud-e Arak River, the route leads to a more desert-like region that resembles the steppes of Central Asia.

You cannot continue northwards after the village of Maraveh Tappeh (above right). There is no access for several hundreds of kilometres along the border with Turkmenistan. The Turkmen, who are semi-nomadic or settled, still live in traditional yurts made of reeds and animal skins.

All the buildings are made using local earth, and are the same colour. There is also a harmony in the volumes. All the dwellings are of the same dimensions and the same structure - a central portico supported by pillars and identical wooden capitals. The buildings for livestock are different; their shapes more varied. The stables, grouped around a central courtyard, have a kind of canopy to protect the animals from the sun and weather, or they are entirely closed.

YEKKEH CHENAR

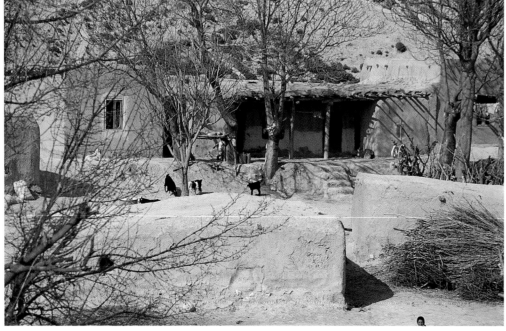

The village of Yekkeh Chenar, to the southeast of Maraveh Tappeh, is characteristic of this region. It is not huddled together like most Iranian villages, but extends down a gentle slope, its houses separated from one another by bushes, hedges or large trees. To this day, nothing has changed its traditional appearance; nothing shocks or stands out.

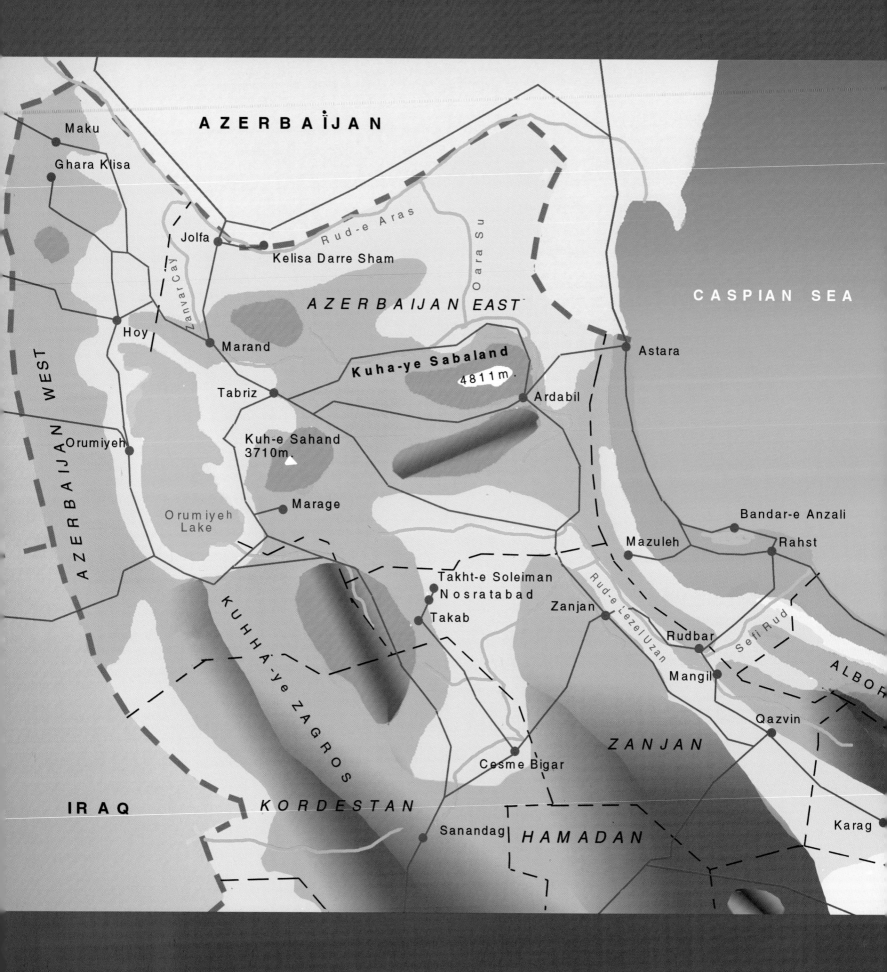

THE NORTH-WEST

Provinces
of
ZANJAN

AZERBAIJAN EAST
and
AZERBAIJAN WEST

The province of **Zanjan** forms a wide corridor to the west of the Alborz Mountains, which leads towards Turkey before crossing the vast plains of **Azerbaijan**.

This region of uneven relief consists of basins (that of Lake Orumiyeh) and mountains of volcanic origin (Mount Sabaland, 4,811 m, the Kuh-e Sahand, 3,710 m). These mountains prevent rainfall, which leads to a dry climate that is cold in winter and temperate in summer.

These lands were part of the Medes' territory, and were known as "Azarpadegan" (Azar - fire, and Padegan - the guardian). There were several sites where fire was guarded, for example the fire temple of Azar Goshmad (200 BC), close to Takab.

The inhabitants, who fled Anatolia at the beginning of the 16th century so as not to fall under the yoke of the Sunni Ottomans, are often of Turkish origin. Their language, Azeri, is still spoken. In the north, the Armenian influence can be felt, with churches of the same style as those found around Erevan and Lake Van in Turkey. To the south, we find the first Kurdish tribes.

The valley of the Rud-e Lezel Uzan river, to the north of Zanjan, has extremely varied landscapes: arid mountains with colours varying from red to ochre (top of the next page) and other more delicate colours, sometimes pastels, especially in autumn. The beauty of these regions of high plateaus lies in their vegetation, which contrasts with the neighbouring deserts. There are still poplars, "the tree of Iran", present. As soon as the slightest stream appears, there are rows of them growing along its banks, or they are found huddled in copses around the farms.

RUDBAR DAM

Water is a great problem in Iran. It rains and snows in the mountains in the north, but the water resulting from the thaw or from storms often runs too rapidly into the Caspian Sea or gets lost in the desert.
The Iranian authorities have built dams in sometimes difficult conditions. The dam (above) located close to the town of Rudbar, between Qazvin and Rusht, on the Sefi Rud, was built in 1961. It is 180 m high and holds back 205 million cubic metres of water.
If we follow the course of the river upstream from the dam, the well-irrigated valley and the warm and humid climate of the region facilitate the cultivation of various crops, rice in particular.

TAKHT-E SOLEIMAN

The site of Takht-e Soleiman, located in the extreme south of Azerbaijan province, not far from the village of Nosratabad, is situated in a stunningly beautiful landscape. A lake with intense blue waters lies in an old volcanic crater. This was an important site for the Sassanians, where the warrior fires were kept burning (see the chapter "Pre-Islamic Iran").

T A K A B

The small village of Takab, in the far south of Azerbaijan province, is approximately 40 kilometres from Takht-e Soleiman.
A few craftsmen still practice their trade in the main street, dying skeins of wool by immersing them in steaming cauldrons.

The road to the northwest of Tabriz, before reaching Ghara Kelisa, crosses a mountainous region with summits as high as 3,600 m. The winters are harsh and the summers torrid. Snow stays on the peaks for several months, but there is little snowfall in the valleys.

Close to Saint Thaddeus Church, "Ghara Kelisa", this pretty village has kept its earthen dwellings intact - nothing spoils the shapes and colours of the traditional-style buildings. The peasant lifestyle remains unchanged - cattle manure is used for heating in winter, and the blocks of dried manure are neatly stacked in the shape of sugar loaves close to the dwellings.

GHARA KELISA

KURDISH VILLAGES

This region is very close to the Turkish border, and the basin of Lake Van. Part of its population of Turkish origin came from Anatolia. They were Shi'ites fleeing the Sunni Ottoman Empire. At that time, Shah Abbas the Great formed a confederation of Turkish-speaking communities.
This decision also attracted a great number of nomads who are now almost all settled in the villages in this area. The Kurdish population mainly established settlements throughout the western parts of Iran, but Kurdish nomads still pass through here. Azeri (a Turkish dialect) is commonly spoken in Azerbaijan.

205

JOLFA

The journey from Tabriz to Jolfa to reach Saint Stephen's church takes you through some beautiful and varied landscapes of mountains, valleys and plains. The neighbouring peaks climb to over 3,000 m and remain snow-capped for much of the year.

The valley of the Zankar Cay river at Marand is renowned for its orchards surrounded by walls of earth (opposite and following pages).

The area around Tabriz in April (above and next page).

A maze of alleyways and rooms with beautiful arches and cupolas branch off the principal gallery, causing narrow shafts of light to illuminate it at oblique angles. There are different types of popular craftwork - the scissors-maker (above) makes scissors from pieces of iron that he smoothes many times on a grinder to craft the tool used to finish carpets.

Fabric stores abound. They sell cloth to those who come from the countryside to stock up. The jewellers' quarter is mostly visited by women who spend a long time gazing into the windows of the tiny shops before deciding to go in.

D own a few steps from the main gallery, you access a big arched room on two levels (above), which is the centre of the carpet trade. There are small boutiques all around where related activities are carried out. Untangling is carried out using machines, but the fringes are finished by hand. Buyers arrive with their pieces of wool, and compare samples to choose the skeins that will be needed for their wives working at home. Accounts are still worked out using an abacus. Tabriz carpets are matte velvet with Ghiordes knots with medallion and corner piece patterns.

The bazaar, with its myriad activities, attracts large crowds. There is a Friday mosque close by, and the mullahs chat outside, or go to their bookseller's stall. There is a workshop where copper is beaten to make cauldrons, and a little further on, friends meet to smoke a "qalian".

To get from Tabriz to Ardabil, then on to the Caspian Sea, it is preferable to take the road that passes north of Mount Sabaland rather than the more direct southern route. The landscapes are grandiose and extremely varied.
After Tabriz, the road climbs up into the mountains, over a summit, then descends towards the long valley of the Oara Su river (above).

MOUNT SABALAND

The north face of the mountain chain is forged out of mineral slopes with ravines in a striking brown-red colour, then a vast area of grassland contrasts with the snow-covered peaks. Earth-coloured villages nestle in the border area between the snowline and the pastures.

The summit of Mount Sabaland, at a height of 4,811 m, is snow-capped and dominates a glacial environment, a far cry from the deserts of central Iran.

217

TURKMENISTAN

Rud e Arak

Maraveh Tappeh
Yekkeh Chenar

Koppe dag

Bognurd

Qucan

CASPIAN SEA

Gonbad-
e Qabus

Azad sar

K U H - e   A L A D A G

Gorgan

Sari

Bastam

Sabzevar

Mashhad

Qaimsahr

Nesapur

Babol

SAH KUH

Sharud

Khorassan

Damghan

K U H - e   S O R B

Semnan

Semnan

D a s h t - e   K e v i r

Kashan

Esfahan

K U H - e   E S G E R

Natanz

Tabas

Ardestan

Nain

Birjand

Esfahan

Yazd

Yazd

Kerman

D a s h t - e   L u t

*Sistan
and
Baluchestan*

Abarkuh

A F G H A N I S T A N

THE NORTH-EAST

Provinces
of
SEMNAN
and
KHORASSAN

The province of **Semnan** covers the south slopes of the Alborz Mountains and their prolongation, the Sah Kuh, then extends across a large area of the Dasht-e Kevir desert. In the northern mountainous parts, the climate is temperate, but the desert parts are excessively hot.

This region has few inhabitants, and they are mostly found close to the Tehran-Mashhad road, above all close to Tehran. This road used to be the caravan route for bypassing the desert before going towards Samarkand.

The neighbouring province of **Khorassan**, the largest in Iran, included a vast territory that it lost in the 19th century following agreements between the Russians and the British - a large part of Afghanistan (Merv and Herat), and Bactriana as far as the Amou Daria River.

The northern territories are very mountainous with rich and abundant flora and fauna, which enabled the creation of the Golestan national park in 1957. Between the mountain chains lies an area of arid steppe.

In the south, there is just the great Dasht-e Lut desert, which runs along the Afghan border. There are few cities, and the largest is Mashhad, which is home for over half the province's population, almost three million inhabitants. There is a flow of pilgrims from all over the world who come to visit the mausoleum of Imam Reza, the "eighth imam of the Shi'ites" in Mashhad. This encouraged the construction of a considerable number of mausoleums and madrasah in the surrounding area, but few have survived the numerous invasions and earthquakes.

Mashhad remained the capital of Iran for a few years only, under the reign of Nadir Shah (1736-1747) of the Afshar tribe. This ruler achieved sweeping victories - he seized Afghanistan, then advanced as far as Delhi in India, from where he brought back the famous Peacock Throne and, after an incursion into Uzbekistan, obtained the capitulation of the Khans of Khiva and Bukhara.

Two renowned mausoleums are found in the area around Mashhad. To the north, at Tus, is that of the poet Ferdowsi, the author of the "Shahnameh", or the Book of Kings, a collection of poems in pure Persian from the Sassanian period; to the west, at Neishabur, is that of the poet and scholar Omar Khayyam.

The region's economy is based on agriculture (sugar beets, wheat, saffron, cotton and fruit), livestock farming, and significant mineral resources, including natural gas at Sarakhs, to the east of Mashhad, close to the Afghan border.

SHAHRUD

The fastest road from Tehran to Mashhad runs alongside the southern slopes of the Alborz Mountains and the vast Dasht-e Kevir desert. This was the trade route taken between Mediterranean ports and Central Asia, as it enabled the caravans to avoid the vast desert in the south, but it also allowed the Turks and Mongols to invade the area.

At Damghan, there are a number of interesting monuments (see the chapter "Islamic Iran"), and the alleys of the old town around the funeral towers are a hive of activity (opposite).

The town of Shahrud (above) is a major stopover point.

On the route from Shahrud to Azad Sar, we can observe the considerable difference in climate and vegetation between the north and south slopes.
The climb up to the peak of Hos Yeilag, at 2,079 m, is through rocky ground and ravines, then we come out into a long, narrow valley (above), which becomes increasingly lush, scattered with small, cultivated plots bordered with rows of poplars.

222

Mashhad, known for its sanctuary and the mausoleum of Khadje Rabi (see previous chapters), is renowned for its avenues, parks and festivals. There are an impressive number of Shi'ite pilgrims - they come from all regions and wear their national costumes.

The Mashhad bazaar stretches through a long two-storey gallery with two parallel aisles. On the first floor, in tiny workshops, craftsmen cut and polish turquoise (top left), others machine-embroider brightly coloured banners. In the boutiques on the ground floor, there are huge quantities of varied articles: perfumes, rosewater, jewellery, headscarves, fabrics, and of course the saffron that grows in the region. Souvenir and religious article sellers for the pilgrims abound - prayer beads and prayer stones sit side by side with copies of the Koran (previous page).

The restaurant, one of the favourite places for Iranians, offers a varied selection of dishes - hors d'œuvres with subtle flavours, a whole range of stews (beef, chicken or mutton) served with sauces with unexpected flavours, rice and yoghurts.
Families sit on low beds, sometimes covered in carpets, and eat listening to music or smoking the "qalian".

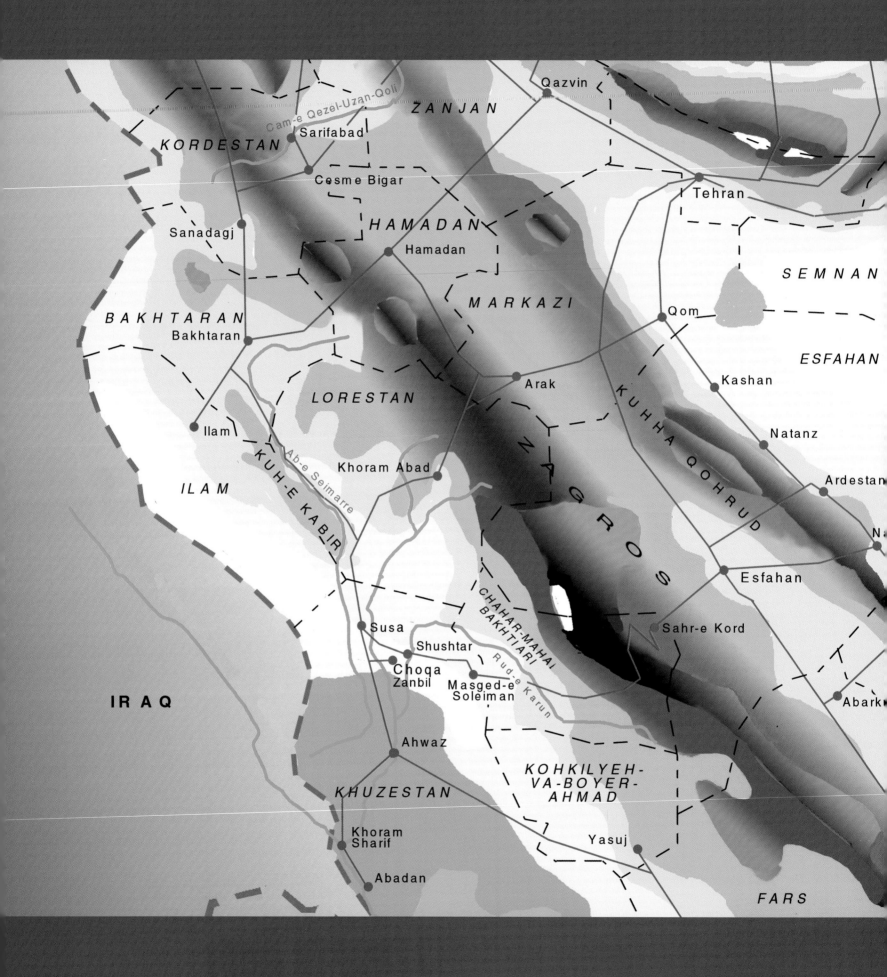

THE WEST

Provinces
of
KORDESTAN
BAKHTARAN
HAMADAN
LORESTAN
ILAM
KHUZESTAN
and
CHAHAR-MAHAL-VA-BAKHTIARI

To the south of Azerbaijan, along the border with Iraq moving southwards, we find the provinces of **Kordestan**, **Bakhtaran**, **Ilam**, and, towards the interior, **Hamadan** and **Lorestan**. This region is almost entirely covered with mountains, with multiple plictations oriented from northwest to southeast, with peaks at around 3,500 m (Kuh-e Alvand) and deep valleys that are sometimes difficult to access.

The climate is very cold, with long winters and snow for almost eight months, but the summers are mild.

The main cities, Hamadan and Bakhtaran, were located on the main through route, the former caravan trail leading from the Mediterranean to Central Asia. This was where the Medes originated, and the sovereigns of the following centuries had scenes telling of their glory carved into the rock.

The inhabitants of different ethic origins, mostly Muslims, retain their own cultures and traditions. Languages spoken include Persian, Turkish, Lor and Kurdish.

Khuzestan is green only during the cold season; as soon as spring arrives, everything is burnt to a crisp.

The Zagros and **Bakhtiari** mountains peter out towards the vast plain that extends as far as the Persian Gulf. These lands are the lowest area in all of Iran.

Like Mesopotamia, this was one of the first places where civilisation became established in the Middle East. Today, the population is of varied origins, though predominantly Arab.

Black gold provides the wealth of the region and the country derives its principal income from it. Around the town of Abadan, there are numerous derricks and huge oil refineries. This province suffered enormously from the Iran-Iraq war; the oil-rich area was subject to repeated attacks, which razed towns and facilities to the ground. The subsequent rebuilding enabled the economic and industrial activities to start up again.

CARAVANSERAI

The Zagros Mountains slope gently across Kordestan province. Today, this region is isolated, far-removed from major communication channels.
In former times, the most frequented routes on the Silk Road came from Baghdad and climbed to the north towards Tabriz, passing alongside Lake Orumyieh. The caravanserai located beside the banks of the Cam-e Qezel-Uzan-Qoli River, close to the village of Sarifabad, was probably a stopping point along this route (above).

Numerous villages are scattered throughout the countryside. The earth houses are of a very regular cube shape, with small, cone-shaped ovens attached to the dwellings.
In this region, the method of storing forage on the terraces of the buildings is quite unique.

AB-E SEIMARRE RIVER

Lorestan province is a high mountainous region with extremely uneven relief.
Torrential rains have created ravines, and the rivers carve out their courses forming impressive canyons (above, the gorges of the Ab-e Seimarre River, to the south-west of Khoram Abad). This land is the domain of the nomads of the Lors tribe.

SHUSHTAR

The province of Khuzestan is close to the Persian Gulf, and the heat is torrid in the summer in the city of Shustar. The Rud-e Karun River that brings water to Shushtar flows into the Gulf at the Iraqi border. It is so hot that the inhabitants have dug out and built underground chambers where they have installed windmills in order to cool down. There are even craftsmen set up underground, like this weaver (next page, bottom left).

Abou Ali (980-1037), known as Avicenne in the West, was born in Bakh in Afghanistan. He lived in Bukhara in Uzbekistan, then in Hamadan, where he died.

He was a great doctor, philosopher, mathematician and poet. His work had a strong influence in the West in the 13th and 14th centuries, up until the 19th century, when it was studied in universities. His mausoleum (above) is topped with a tower similar to that at Gonbad-e Qabus.

From the Zagros Mountains, with peaks at 3,000 m, we descend towards the plains of Susiana, discovering grandiose but austere landscapes, carved out by the upper valley of the Rud-e Karun River and its affluents. The plain of Mesopotamia stretches westwards to the Iraqi border. This region is important because of the development of the Sumerian and Babylonian cultures, of which the Ziggurat at Choqa-Zanbil are the best-preserved remains (below right).

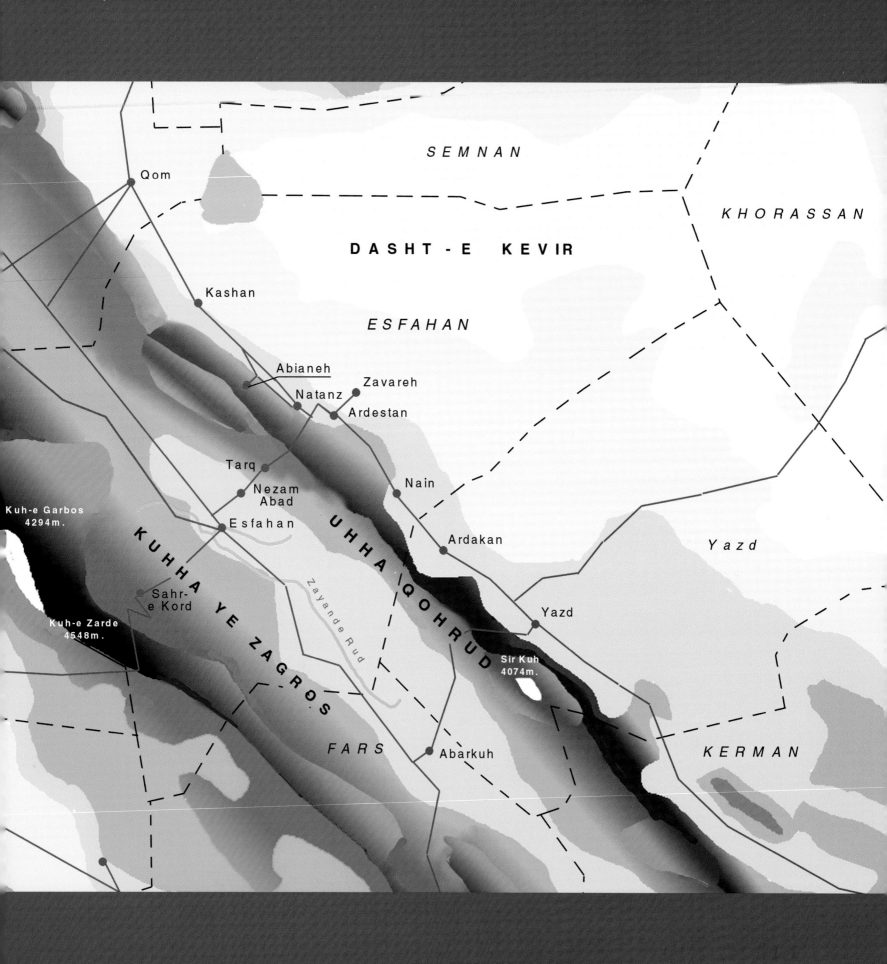

SEMNAN

KHORASSAN

DASHT - E KEVIR

Qom

Kashan

ESFAHAN

Abianeh

Zavareh

Natanz

Ardestan

Tarq

Nain

Nezam
Abad

Esfahan

UHHA

Kuh-e Garbos
4294m.

QOHRUD

Ardakan

Yazd

Sahr-
e Kord

Zayande Rud

KUHHA YE ZAGROS

Yazd

Kuh-e Zarde
4548m.

Sir Kuh
4074m.

FARS

Abarkuh

KERMAN

THE CENTRE

Provinces
of
ESFAHAN
and
YAZD

Esfahan and the surrounding areas have often been described by a number of renowned writers, such as Pierre Loti, Teilhard de Chardin, Jeanne Dieulafoy, Robert Byron and Gobineau. They were all fascinated by the region's deserts, mountains and well-irrigated oases.

Water has always been the principal concern of those ruling the region. They irrigated the plain with the Zayendeh Rud River, "the life-giving river".

The temperate climate is due to the plains, situated at an altitude of 1,430 m, and the height of the surrounding mountains.

The caravan routes traversed these oases before crossing the Zagros and Qohrud mountains in the direction of Shiraz and the Persian Gulf, or the north and the east towards Uzbekistan and India.

The great invaders Tamerlane and Gengis Khan reached this far, but the city escaped disaster several times.

The Seljuk dynasty, in the 11th century, gave the first great boost to Esfahan by making it their capital. A number of buildings still bear witness to this. Then, Shah Abbas I, with all the building work he had done, made Esfahan one of the world's most beautiful capitals.

The province of Yazd is covered for the most part with great swathes of the Dasht-e Lut desert and the Qohrud mountain chain, which stretches from northwest to southeast.

A major road runs along the north face of these mountains, bordered with a few oases fed with water running down from the summits. For centuries, a significant flow of traffic has travelled this route. Marco Polo went through Yazd on his way to China, and described it as "a great and noble city", and its inhabitants, as they are to this day, as "honest and hardworking".

Kashan is a veritable oasis that stretches between Mount Kuhha, which has peaks at 3,500 m, and the torrid desert of Dasht-e Kevir. The "qanats", indicated by giant mounds of earth, provide water for the town, thus feeding the abundant vegetation that surrounds the houses. The Bagh-e Fin garden (below) is open to the public, and large numbers of people come to enjoy the coolness next to the marble canals through which abundant clear water cascades.

S everal public and private buildings are worth visiting in Kashan. These include the Agha Bozorg Museum (below), the Borujerdi House (above), Tabatabei House (right) and other monuments described in the first part of this book.

The charming dale of the Barz Rud River, in the Kuhha Mountains between Kashan and Natanz, leads to the small village of Abianeh.
Orchards and cultivated fields are dotted along the watercourse, in the middle of clusters of trees of various species, which lend the autumn a rich palette of colours broken occasionally by the turquoise domes of mausoleums. There is a striking contrast between this bucolic panorama and the desert we left a few dozen kilometres behind.

242

Here, the poplars permeate the landscape with their colours, or blend in with the red ochre of the earth that covers the walls of the houses. Poplars take over from the palm trees found in the desert. These trees are precious - their wood is used to build the floors of the terraces of the mud houses, handles for farming tools, draw bars for carts, and to build culverts over the mountain torrents.

The apricots drying on the terraces add yet more bright colours to the surroundings (next page).

ABIANEH

The inhabitants of Abianeh have ancient ties with the Zoroastrian communities that emigrated to India and Pakistan, and have retained, despite thirteen centuries of Islam, their dialect and their traditional costume, consisting of large flowery headscarves and aprons over black dresses for the women, and skullcaps, and puffed black jackets and trousers for the men. The houses have many floors and latticed wooden balconies, and are covered in red ochre earth.

On the route from Natanz to Esfahan, remains remind us that this was a route followed by travellers in ancient times. In Tarq (above), there is an ancient caravanserai whose walls are gradually disintegrating with time, and further on at Nezam Abad, we find the ramparts of a fortified village (below).

SAFFRON

The cultivation of the crocus, used to make saffron, takes place in various parts of Iran, in particular here, between Natanz and Esfahan. The purple flowers are picked one by one at the beginning of the autumn. Great care is taken to keep the three pistils, which are then dried or ground to produce the yellow-orange powder that is so prized.

Saffron is expensive because 100,000 flowers are needed to produce just one kilo of this precious product.

It is commonly used to flavour dishes, and in the pharmaceutical industry.

On the borders of the Dasht-e Kevir desert, the small town
of Ardestan is entirely earth-coloured. Life has survived
in this arid environment due to the water supply via "qanats",
underground channels that bring the water from the mountains to
the oasis.

The small town of Nain, also located at the gateway to the desert, owes its world-wide reputation to the carpet weaving carried out in its modest households.

Life is peaceful here, and it is not unusual to encounter elderly men sat on the ground talking and spinning wool to be used by the women to make the carpets in the shade of the majestic wind towers.

The loom, a large wooden frame, takes up considerable space in a room set aside for the purpose. The woman checks the card (top left), which shows her the details of the pattern and the colours to use. Various skeins of wool are hung above the area where she works, enabling her to choose the desired thread. The Senneh knot is created without a needle (above), and leaves only a single thread visible. There may be between 2,000 and 10,000 knots per square decimetre for a carpet, which makes the design extremely sophisticated.

When a row is finished, it is tightened using a metal comb, then shaved with special scissors (below).

One person working alone takes around eight months to make a carpet of 3 m by 4 m.

The town of Nain has beautiful residences dating from the Safavid period. Despite the demolition undertaken to modernise the town, there are still a few remarkable houses.
Around a rectangular courtyard decorated with a pond and fountain, the various split-level rooms open out onto a gallery.

The routes that converge on Esfahan from the north or the southeast are former caravan trails dotted with abandoned caravanserais, most of them in ruins. They were all built to the same square plan, with a richly decorated tower at each corner and a single monumental entry gate.

ESFAHAN

Esfahan is a beautiful oasis surrounded by greenery. It spreads out at the foot of the mountains at an altitude of 1,430 m, which gives it a relatively gentle climate. The view from its terraces is striking due to the uniformity of the colours and volumes. Only the most beautiful monuments stand out - minarets like those of Ali, and the cupolas of the Imam, Sheikh Lotfollah and Friday mosques, for example.

The city is very lively, and the people enjoy going to meeting places, such as the "chaikhaneh" at Khaju bridge, where the young and the old mix.

In Iran, every town has at least one "house of power", known as the "zurkhaneh", where the men, the "pahlavani", come to train every evening. It is a kind of religious brotherhood.

The square room is built like a pit surrounded by mirrors so that all the exercises can be observed. The leader is placed to one side on a raised platform, and provides the rhythm with a drum and chants to encourage the players. The public, on stands opposite one another, take part by applauding.

One of the main exercises consists of juggling in rhythm with wooden clubs that weigh up to 60 kg.

The imperial bazaar, the "Qaisaryehw" opens onto the Royal Square opposite the Mosque of the Shah. Its gate, built under Shah Abbas the Great, leads to a large, main alley with an arched ceiling, which is the starting point for a labyrinth of small side streets and rooms. The whole complex was formerly covered with arched ceilings and cupolas as far as the Mosque of Ali.

The bazaar is full of hand-crafted products: carved trays (below), tools for carpet weaving (opposite), tablecloths with prints made using woodblocks ("qalemkars"), and beautiful carpets (next page).

The copper foundry district is based in a large arched alley, perpendicular to the Royal Square, behind the Ali Qapu palace. Going there is like stepping back in time. Copper is beaten to make objects of all sizes and for all uses - vases, ewers, trays, huge cauldrons, etc.

The object is shaped while held in place by the craftsman's foot or placed on a strange-shaped wooden platform. The noise is deafening.

TOWARDS YAZD

Before reaching Yazd, the further east you go, staying between the mountains and the desert, the more arid the landscape becomes. There are however still a few villages lined up along the points where water is to be found.
The linear profile of these groups of dwellings is broken by more vertical buildings that are recognisable from a distance - grain stores, wind towers and domes close to the ground over ventilated reservoirs.

The Sir Kuh mountain chain (which climbs to 4,074 m) dominates Yazd, and serves as the city's water tower. A network of almost 50 km of "qanats" provides water. This ancient city hides under terraces and domes from which minarets and a large number of wind towers emerge. Most dwellings are ventilated this way, since the climate here, near the desert, is harsh. The wind towers direct the slightest breath of cool air captured inside the rooms.

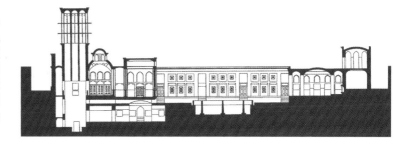

Yazd has a large Zoroastrian community. Zarathustra preached this religion in the 6th century BC. Zoroastrian beliefs are based on the recognition of a supreme God, Ahura Mazda. The "sacred fire" is the image of this God. It is constantly maintained in a large bronze bowl in a room that only the great priest is allowed to enter. He has to wear a mask so his breath does not sully the fire. Outside the city, the bodies of the dead used to be exposed on the towers of silence (above and next page) to be devoured by vultures. The priest then threw their bones into a well at the centre of the top of the tower. This practice was outlawed 50 years ago for reasons of hygiene.

I n a tiny back street in the outskirts of Yazd, huge stones over two metres in diameter (opposite) stand alongside the pavement. This is the henna mills quarter. The leaves of the henna bush are ground into very fine powder using these huge millstones, which are controlled by an engine that turns around a circular platform. Other millstones crush rape seed. The mixture is used to dye and strengthen men's beards and women's hair.

The monumental façade of the Takieh-e Mir bazaar, with three rows of arcades topped with two minarets, is reflected in a long ornamental pond, which makes it look larger. It was built at the end of the 19th century, during the Qadjar period, and is only for show now, since the true bazaar in Yazd is elsewhere, close to the small streets of the old town.

The arches, or simply the curved porticos in the maze of covered passages create a constant play of light and shadow.

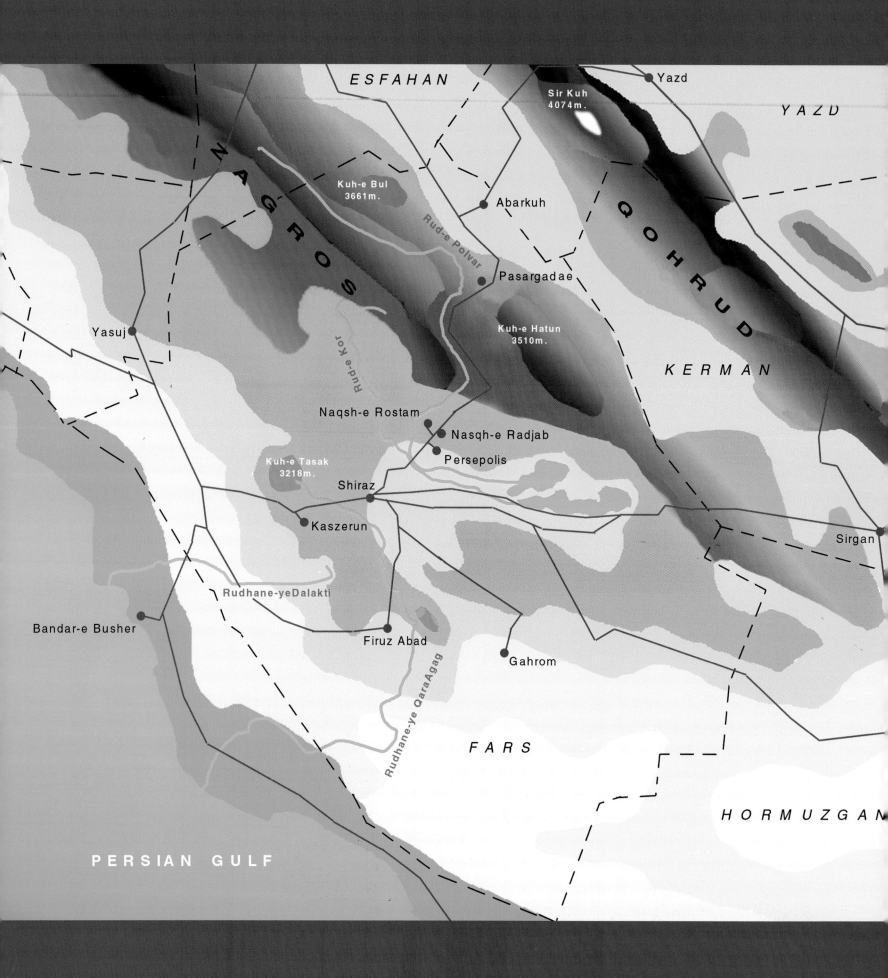

ESFAHAN

YAZD

Yazd

Sir Kuh
4074m.

QOHRUD

ZAGROS

Kuh-e Bul
3661m.

Rud-e Polvar

Abarkuh

Pasargadae

Kuh-e Hatun
3510m.

KERMAN

Yasuj

Rud-e Kor

Naqsh-e Rostam

Nasqh-e Radjab

Persepolis

Kuh-e Tasak
3218m.

Shiraz

Kaszerun

Sirgan

Rudhane-yeDalakti

Bandar-e Busher

Firuz Abad

Gahrom

Rudhane-ye QaraAgag

FARS

HORMUZGAN

PERSIAN GULF

THE SOUTH-WEST

FARS
Province

Most of Iran's geographical and historical features are to be found in the province of Fars. Iran used to be known as Fars, "Persia", and its language was called "Farsi".

Fars province is a mountainous land, with the Zagros Mountains, with its steppes and fertile valleys occupying a large proportion of the territory.

The snow-capped peaks (Kuh-e Hatun, 3,510 m, Kuh-e Bul, 3,661 m) temper the climate. There is little precipitation and water resources are scarce, except for the water that runs down from the mountains. The course of the river Kol, which crosses the province, is controlled by a series of dams forming freshwater lakes, which play an important role in the water balance of the region.

Fars was the land chosen by the Achaemenids; it later witnessed the emergence and flourishing of the Sassanians. They left monuments behind that are known worldwide, and there are probably many more as yet unknown.

After several centuries of silence, the Zend dynasty once again made Fars the centre of the Empire in the 18th century.

The landscapes are austere, the red-brown, greenish and ochre earth of the bare mountains is no longer that of Pasargadae, which was resplendent with gardens and flowers during the period of its greatness; in former times the plain of Persepolis was a vast garden.

This is the land of the Qashqais, nomads who make their livelihoods from breeding livestock. In the summer, they live in the mountains to the west of Shiraz, and in winter, they move down to the pastures in Khusestan province.

Shiraz, whose name trips gently off the tongue, still cultivates its image as a "city of roses and poets" (and formerly of wine). It stands at an altitude of 1,600 m, and is dominated to the south by peaks of almost 3,400 m. The climate is pleasant in winter and bearable in summer. Shiraz, surrounded by flowers and greenery, has some remarkable monuments (see descriptions in the first part of this book). They include the Nasir al Molk (right) and Va Atiq (below) mosques, the Shah Cherag mausoleum (above), the Bagh-e Eram gardens and a citadel right in the town centre (previous page).

The greatest Persian poet, Chams ed Din Mohammed (1324-1388), named "Hafez" (he who knows the Koran by heart), lies in the middle of a garden planted with cypress and orange trees. His work is known to all, and even the least literate Iranian can quote a few verses. Anyone opening his anthology, the Divan, at random is said to be able to read his or her future there.

Here lies Moucharrif ed Din Shirazi, known as Sa'adi, born in Shiraz in 1190. He is said to have lived to a hundred. He travelled extensively, and was even captured by the Crusaders.
He is the poet who wrote the "Golestan" (The Rose Garden), the "Bustan" (The Orchard) and the "Pend Nameh" (Book of Advice), which have been translated into English.

The bazaar of the Regent, the "bazaar-e Vakil", named after the regent who created it in the 17th century, is close to the mosque of the same name. Its arched architecture is remarkable in terms of the solidity and the decorative aspect of its bricks.

Numerous tiny alleys give onto the main street or onto squares with ancient caravanserais surrounded by small boutiques where you can buy hand-crafted goods (above). And of course, there is the district where the carpets for which Shiraz is renowned are sold.

The anniversary of the death of the martyr Imam Hussein, who died in Kerbala, the Ashura, is celebrated on the 10th of Moharram (the first month of the Islamic year).
A great deal of preparation goes into this occasion, which makes the bazaars particularly animated. The people rush to buy objects to be used for the processions - flags, hangings, whips, costumes, musical instruments, etc. Over several days, processions of men, dressed in black and floats stream along the streets of the city to the rhythm of the drums.

The area around Shiraz in Fars province is the birthplace of two of the greatest Persian dynasties - the Achaemenids and the Sassanians.
The most grandiose site is undoubtedly Persepolis (above, and described in the first part of this book). Darius the Great, who had abandoned Pasargadae, the former capital of Fars (below right), had a sumptuous palace built there.
A few kilometres from Persepolis, the tombs of the Achaemenid and Sassanian kings (below left) are carved into the cliffs at Naqsh-e Rostam.

The plains of Fars province are surrounded by mountains in a desert climate, whose peaks rise to over 3,500 m (the Kuh-e Bul, 3,661 m and the Kuh-e Hatun, 3,510 m). The "qanats" that start from the foot of the mountains are sometimes dug up to 20 or 30 metres below ground to channel water to villages or oases dozens of kilometres away. They are recognisable due to the line of giant mounds of earth, which correspond to aeration and access ducts crowned with stones resulting from digging or maintenance of the underground network. This system of irrigation still provides water resources for a large number of people.

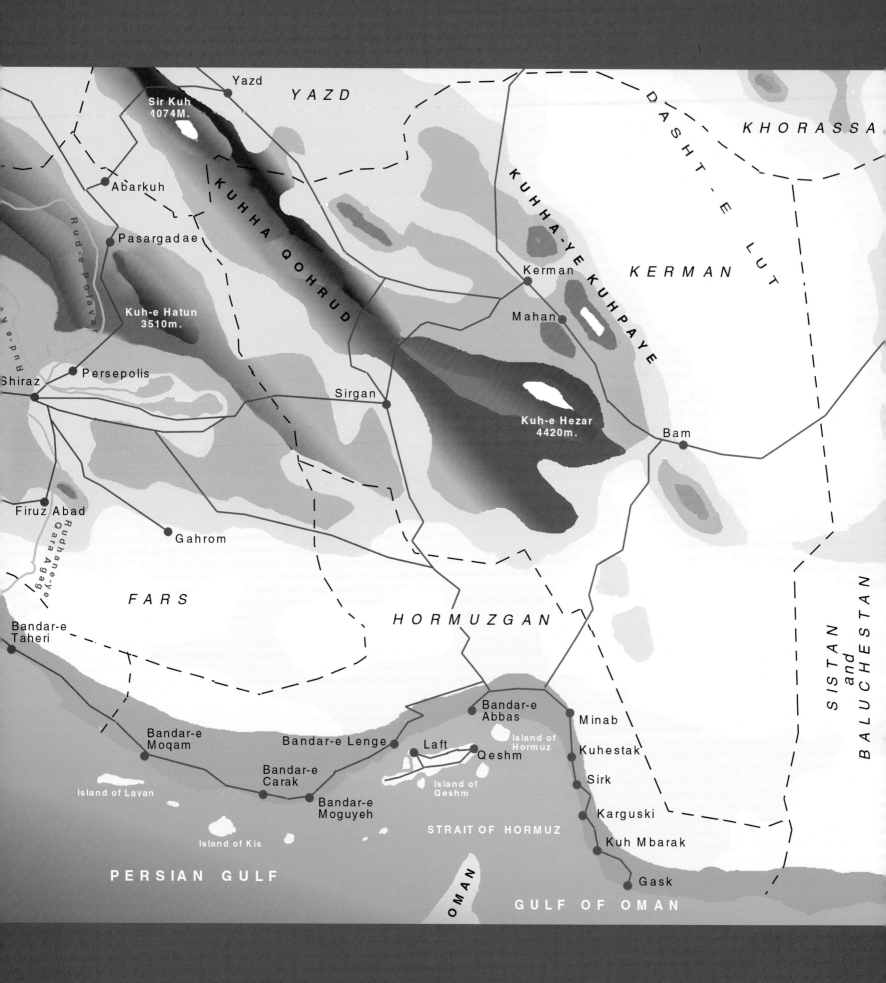

THE SOUTH

Provinces
of
KERMAN
and
HORMUZGAN

The province of **Kerman** is a region of arid lands with a tropical climate in stark contrast with the northern regions. The eastern part of the province is an extension of the Lut desert, and the west is the end of the Qohrud Mountains, with high, often snow-capped peaks (Kuh-e Hezar at 4,420 m).

The Halil Rud, a permanent river that crosses the province, is the largest watercourse, but the province lacks water despite the irrigation arrangements and the subterranean channels, or "qanats". This means that the population density is low. The language spoken is Persian, and the population is mostly Muslim, with a Zoroastrian minority.

The crops cultivated are characteristic of hot dry regions - sugar beets, cumin, cotton, lemons, pistachios and dates, with the latter two products grown for export. The open copper mines south of the town of Rafsanjan are the largest in the world.

There was significant caravan traffic between India and the Persian Gulf under the reign of the Safavids, but the Afghans and the Baluch then contributed to the impoverishment of this region, which took a long time to recover.

The province of **Hormuzgan** extends along the length of the Persian Gulf, the Strait of Hormuz and the Gulf of Oman. It is located at a low altitude, and its climate is very hot and humid with little precipitation. The town of Bandar-e Abbas was taken by the Portuguese Alfonso of Albuquerque, who founded a trading post there in 1514 as a base for the route to India. In 1622, Shah Abbas the Great succeeded in taking back this territory with the help of the English. The town's port is still thriving today. It is Iran's major port, with over 50% of the country's goods traffic. The island of Kis, which formerly belonged to the Arabs, was known for its particularly beautiful pearls.

This region remains in a particularly sensitive strategic position today, and should become a tourist centre in the years to come. Projects for the islands of Qeshm and Kis are currently under examination.

KERMAN

The Fianjalli Khan hammam, located right in the centre of the bazaar, is perfectly conserved. The out-of-kilter entrance hall leads to a large room consisting of six vestibules around a bathing pool.

People undressed and relaxed here before going to the various small rooms for massages and hot and cold baths.

The structures (beams, capitals, ribbed roofs) are well proportioned, and the mosaic decoration adds to the relaxing atmosphere of the place.

In a small mosque close to the bazaar entrance, near the Friday mosque, a mullah addresses the faithful at the approach to the anniversary of Hussein's death. There is deep meditation, hardly broken by the waiter handing glasses of tea to those present.

At this time of year, the boutiques in the bazaar overflow with all sorts of items (caps, whips of all sizes, chain mail waistcoats, musical instruments, etc.), that are purchased by those participating in the processions.

MAHAN

The oasis of Mahan is nestled in a vale in the mountains of the desert, whose summits reach almost 4,000 metres. Winter brings the most striking colour contrasts, with the snow-covered mountains, the arid valley, and the green oasis, from which a few small ochre-coloured earth cupolas appear.

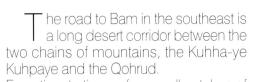

The road to Bam in the southeast is a long desert corridor between the two chains of mountains, the Kuhha-ye Kuhpaye and the Qohrud.
From time to time, a few small patches of green created by tiny oases are found, they owe their existence to the supply of water from the mountains provided by the "qanats".

293

Bam (previous page), considered Iran's most beautiful oasis, is renowned for its oranges and its fleshy, tasty dates. From the top of the citadel, the viewpoints behind the battlements in the ramparts are different. On one side, stretching to the horizon, is the palm grove irrigated by the "qanats", on the other is the vastness of the desert, represented by the succession of mountains each with a different colour, gradually fading into the distance.

The landscapes are highly uneven between Bam and Bandar-e Abbas. There are a succession of mountain chains cut across by desert plains. The peaks get lower moving down towards the Strait of Hormuz, but the rocks become increasingly sharp.

Around Bandar-e Abbas, the desperately flat coast is drained by the delta of several rivers, usually dry. The climate is very hot and humid. In the area adjacent to the mountains, in the hinterland, a few flourishing palm groves, like the one at Minab, produce excellent dates. In this region, women do not cover their faces with veils; they wear masks made of leather or embroidered fabric in various colours (they can be black, or even bright red). The masks allow air to circulate and stop the fabric from sticking to the skin.

The island of Qeshm (Jazireh-e Qeshm), situated in the strait of Hormuz between the Persian Gulf and the Gulf of Oman, is Iran's largest island at 100 km in length.
It is dreary and flat with no vegetation. A few tiny hills of whitish earth rise up here and there to break the monotony.
The climate is torrid, sometimes slightly attenuated by the humid air from the ocean, but this makes the atmosphere considerably more oppressive.

All along the desperately flat north coast, there are isolated dhow building workshops. The beams and planks used are carved with rudimentary tools. The construction methods and the shapes of these boats have not changed for centuries. The frame is still as robust and the caulking is extremely important to ensure that the hull is watertight, in particular due to the heat, which strains the entire structure. This hulk of wood is an impressive sight when at sea.

The island and its main town, located in the extreme northeast, are known by the same name. Its status as a free port means that a lot of activity takes place here. Merchandise arrives from abroad in transit, and many Iranians come to make purchases of household and audio-visual goods in particular.

In Laft, in the north of the island, a lagoon is used as an anchorage for dhows, which are lined up in the direction of the current.
The simple cube-shaped dwellings all possess their own wind towers. This enables them to draw maximum benefit from the sea breeze, as the heat is torrid during the day all year round.

The shape of the dhows is just as beautiful whether they are at sea or in dry docks for careening.
These boats are used for fishing, and for the daily service between the island and the mainland.
Faster ferries and hovercraft are gradually replacing them.

Prehistoric troglodyte dwellings were dug into these hills of whitish tuff. Later, their inhabitants used them to remain under the protection of the Portuguese fortified city established at the summit.

Water is scarce on the island, and the villages have tanks and public wells. Here in Laft, several have been dug within a small area. The women, wearing their masks, come every day to collect the water needed for their households.

The climate and the type of soil vary enormously from region to region. We move from a plain, where conditions are suitable for growing cotton, directly to arid and barren land where salt springs from the ground in a torrent.

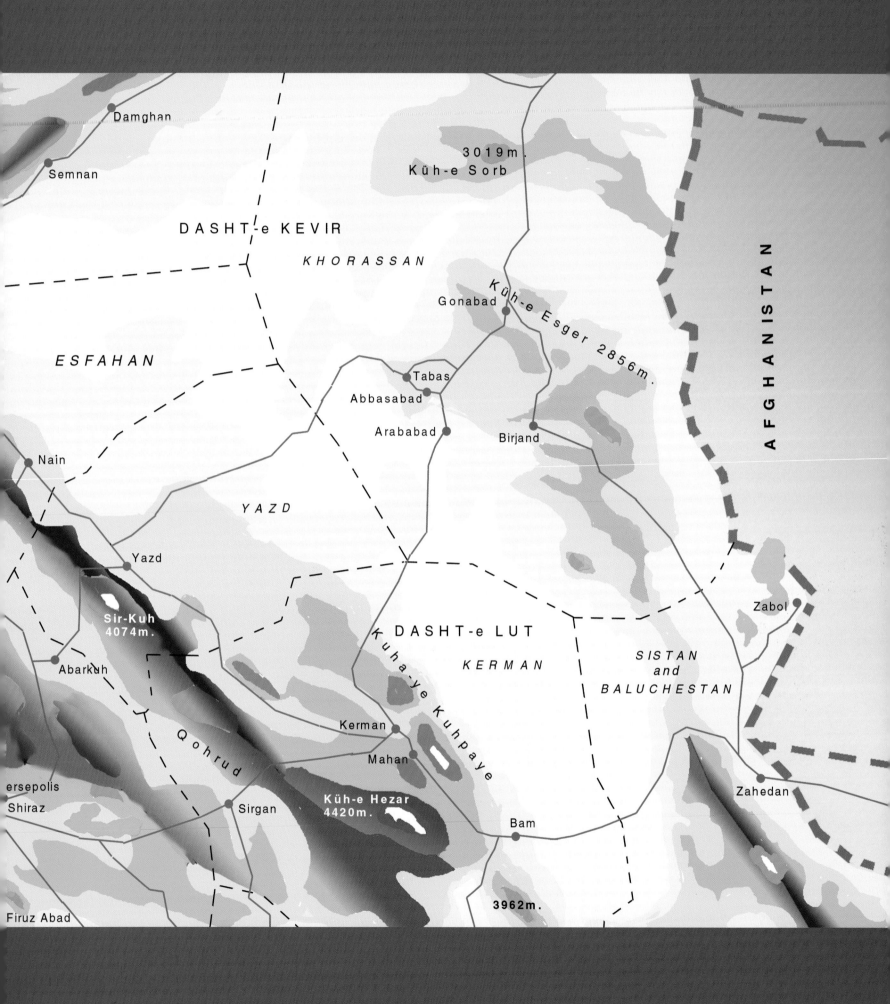

THE DESERTS

DASHT-E KEVIR
DASHT-E LUT

The centre of Iran is a vast desert surrounded by high mountain chains, which prevent precipitation from falling. In the north, several watercourses flow into the **Dasht-e Kevir**. Their water disappears into the lands gorged with salt and impracticable mud lakes. The largest of them, the Darya-ye Namak, is located around 100 km south of Tehran, at an altitude of 765 m.

This immense territory can be crossed from the city of Yazd in the direction of Tabas. The nature of the soil varies: there are sand dunes, salty crusts and reddish earth.

In the west and southwest, the **Dasht-e Lut**, at a lower altitude (an average of 300 m) has a much more torrid climate.

A tarmac-covered road leads northwards from Kerman to cross the Kuhha-ye Kuhpaye, passing through extremely beautiful landscapes. The earth is highly coloured, in an infinite variety of shades of red - the reliefs are structured with varied shapes and lines.

A few ancient caravanserais are still dotted along the routes of the caravans that used to cross this vast Iranian desert, going from oasis to oasis. Today, lorries have replaced dromedaries, which are still part of the landscape, however; great herds can be seen foraging in this arid universe, as they are still indispensable for those inhabitants who do not possess motor vehicles.

Tabas, the largest oasis in these deserts, has date palms and orchards. It suffered enormously from an earthquake in 1968, as did the oasis of Ferdous. Almost all of the traditional dwellings with terraces, cupolas and thick walls of raw earth were destroyed.

THE KUHHA-YE KUHPAYE

Until recent years, the deserts in central Iran were accessible only by trails. The journey from Kerman to Mashhad can now be undertaken without difficulty. In the first part of the journey, the landscapes are magnificent, a magical world of colour.

A few well-conserved caravanserais are still dotted along this route, which was taken by the caravans of the Silk Road.

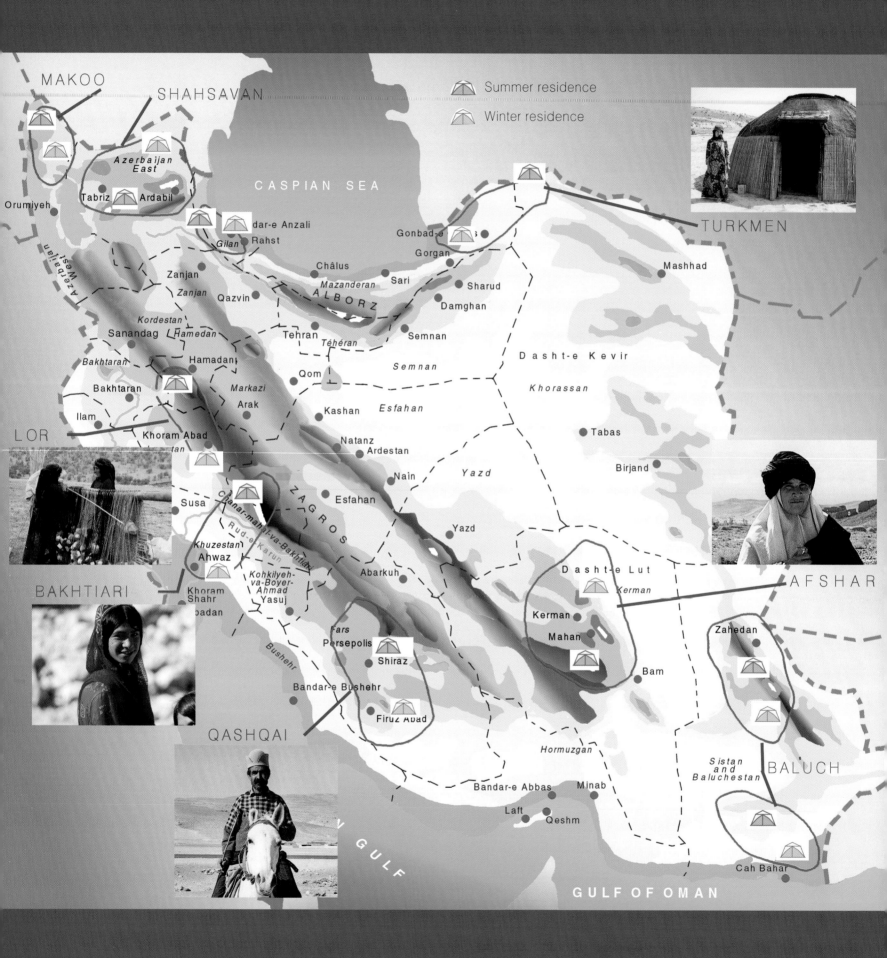

NOMADS

The population of Iran has constantly changed over the centuries with the migration of peoples who have crossed its lands. Most of its peoples came from Central Asia, with the Turkish and Mongol tribes, then from the west, with the Greeks and then the Arabs.

Some minorities have kept their customs, languages and traditional ways of life. They are nomads who live from breeding goats and sheep. The policy of forced sedentarisation carried out at the beginning of the 20th century modified the lives of these groups, but these cultural differences are now tolerated, and some tribes of nomads still carry out transhumance between summer and winter pastures.

The various tribes are spread all around the Iranian plateau, living between plains and mountains:

- The **Makoos**, in the province of Azerbaijan West, live in tents.
- The **Shahsavans** and the **Arasbarans**, in Azerbaijan, have yurts covered with animal skins and travel by camel. Their carpets are not well known.

- The **Shandermans** and the **Khashehbaris**, from Gilan province, live in little wooden huts.
- The **Bakhtiaris**, from Chahar-Mahal-va-Bakhtiari province, live in tents. They travel by horse. They are renowned for their carpets.
- The **Lors**, in Lorestan, have tents in woven canvas and plaited reeds and travel by mule.
- The **Qashqais**, in Fars province, live in canvas tents and carry out transhumance on horses and donkeys. They weave beautiful carpets.
- The **Afshars**, in Kerman province, live in tents. They produce beautiful carpets.
- The **Baluch**, in Sistan province, build earth yurts covered with thatch. They are renowned for their carpets.
- The **Kurds**, in Khorassan, also live in tents and travel by camel.
- The **Turkmen**, in Mazanderan province, have collapsible yurts with reeds for walls, covered with stretched animal skins.

The Lors nomads' principal territories are in Bakhtaran and Lorestan provinces.
During the summer, they let their herds graze in the mountains of the Kuhha-ye Zagros, to the north of Bakhtaran. In autumn, they drive them down to the warm regions to the south of Khoram-Abad to spend the winter. There are about two and a half million of them, and their language is similar to Old Persian.

The Bakhtiari nomads spend summer in the Zagros Mountains to the west of Esfahan, in the area surrounding the village of Shahr-e Kord in Chahar-Mahal-va-Bakhtiari province. They have a long way to travel to reach their winter encampments near Ahwaz in Khuzestan. There are around six hundred thousand of these shepherds, and they speak Farsi. The women, draped in brightly coloured, often red, fabrics, stand proud. The men wear the "chooga", a type of white kimono with wide black stripes, and small dark-coloured skullcaps.

The Qashqais live in Fars province. They spend the summer to the north of Shiraz, close to the village of Ardakan, in pastures at an altitude of 3,000 m.

They come down before winter, obtain a few supplies in Shiraz after selling the carpets they have made, then establish their camp to the south of Firuz Abad. This makes a trip of a total of almost 300 km.

This population, of which there are estimated to be three hundred thousand, is constantly dwindling.

The grey or beige felt hat is the only distinctive sign that remains for the men. The women, however, wear several dresses on top of one another, in bright colours or with floral patterns. The overall effect is harmonious as they move forward on their mounts while spinning wool.

The Qashqai's tents are scattered around the pastures where they have stopped. The tents aren't grouped together because each family keeps its independence. During the day, the canvas is removed, the blankets and rugs are carefully folded, and, close by, the women prepare the meal - tea and nan bread. With great dexterity, they knead the dough, and roll it using a thin stick to obtain a thin flat shape. They then cook it over a wood fire.

THE AFSHARS

The Afshars are nomads who move around extensively. They live in several provinces of Iran: Azerbaijan, to the east of Lake Orumiyeh, Hamadan, and in the south of Kerman (opposite) during the summer. They move down towards Bandar-e Abbas to spend the winter there.
The women wear an odd, large black turban high on their heads.

THE TURKMEN

The Turkmen, who arrived in northeast Iran around the 11th century, live in Mazanderan province. In summer, they occupy the pasturelands in the Sah-Kuh Mountains, and in winter, they move down to the region of Maraveh Tappeh. Today, they are almost all sedentary, but they still live in their yurts for nostalgia's sake (below).

Turkmen

Turkmen

Turkmen

Yazd

Turkmen

Turkmen

Turkmen

Kurd

Kurd

Afghan

Tehran

Abianeh

Mazuleh

Yazd

Mashhad

Bandar-e Abbas

Abianeh

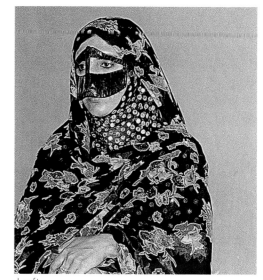

Laft

Bakhtiari

Nain

Turkmen

Esfahan

Lor

Lor

Qashqai

Qashqai

Qashqai

Lor

Bakhtiari

Lor

INDEX

GLOSSARY

Apadana	Court room or throne room of the Persians of Antiquity.
Bandar	Port.
Chador	Literally means "tent". A veil, usually black, which covers women from head to foot when they go out in public.
Goldatesh	In Iran, small aedicule with a wooden structure and pyramid-shaped roof erected on the central iwan enabling the imam to address the crowd of worshippers assembled in the courtyard.
Gonbad	*Gounbad*, or *Gonbed*, *Kouba*. Dome and cupola in Turkey and Iran, mausoleum in the shape of a tower.
Haft rangi	Ceramic on which a pattern has been painted before firing (7 colours).
Hypostyle	Describes a room where the ceiling is supported by columns.
Imam	In Sunni Islam, the imam leads prayers in the mosque. In Shi'ite Islam, the imam is a descendent of the Prophet who interprets the Koran.
Imamzadeh	In Iran, the tomb of Shi'ite imams.
Iwan	*Eivan* in Iran, *Liwan* in India. Rectangular room, usually with an arched ceiling, and open to the outside on one side only. Originally from Persia (Sassanian). Can also be an element of profane architecture.
Khaneqah	*Khanaga* or *Hanaga*. Convent, generally located next to a mosque.
Kelisa	Church.
Madrasah	In Iran. *Medersa* in Morocco and Tunisia, also called *madrassa* (Egypt) and *medressi* (Turkey). The root of the word is "to study". Establishment usually for higher studies in theology and law. Often attached to a mosque.
Mihrab	Sometimes written *mehrab*. Niche in a wall to indicate that it is the *qibla* (showing the direction of Mecca for prayers). The niche is usually richly decorated.
Menar	Minaret (term used in Iran and India).
Minbar	Pulpit from which the imam gives the sermon in a mosque.
Masdjed	*Masjid* (Arabic), *masjed* (India and Iran), *mesjed* (Tunisia), *camii* (Turkey), *mezquita* (Spain). Building where Muslims gather for prayer. Friday mosques are those where all the believers gather for the sermon and prayer on Fridays.
Mouquarna	*Muqarna*, or *stalactite*. Angle squinch enabling the switch from square to circular, particularly for building cupolas.
Naos	Main inside part of a temple.
No Ruz	Iranian new year (from March 21st to 24th)
Pichtag	Entrance iwan (huge gate) to a mosque. Higher than the walls surrounding it.
Pol	Bridge.
Qalian	Nargileh. Large pipe with a flexible tube and a reservoir of perfumed water.
Qânât	Underground channel to bring water from the mountains to villages.
Qibla	Or *qebla*. Direction of Mecca, pointing towards the "Ka'ba". This is the wall in which the mihrab niche is set. It shows the direction worshippers should face to pray.
Rud	River.
Tepe	Artificial hill.
Zaouia	Mausoleum for a holy man, marabout in the Maghreb.
Zelliges	These consist of small ceramic tiles in different colours that have been carved, often according to a very specific design, in slabs of unified shades. These fragments are then assembled to create the overall pattern and sealed with mortar.

BIBLIOGRAPHY

Amiet P., *Suse, 6000 ans d'histoire*, Musée du Louvre, 1988
Baharnaz M.R., *Nomads of Iran*, Fahrang-Sara Publications, 1994
Bailhache Alain, *Ispahan, l'espace voilé du désir*, Yassavoli, 1995
Bartol V, *Alamut*, Phébus, 1988
Beny Roloff, *Persia, Bridge of Turquoise*, Fahrang-Sara Publications, 1993
Bird, Isabella, *Journeys in Persia and Kurdistan*, London, John Murray, 1891
Boyle J., *Persia: History and Heritage*, Allen and Unwin, 1978
Briant P., *Alexandre the Great*, Thames & Hudson, 1996
Briant P., *Darius, les Perses et l'Empire*, Gallimard, 1992
Byron Robert, *The Road to Oxiana*, Penguin, 1992
Chardin J., *Travels in Persia, 1673-1677*, Dover Publications, 1988
Dieulafoy Jeanne, *Une Amazone en Orient, du Caucase à Persépolis, 1881-1882*, Phébus, 1989
Dieulafoy Jeanne, *En mission chez les immortels, fouilles de Suse en 1884-1886*, Phébus, 1990
Dieulafoy Jeanne, *L'Orient sous le voile de Shiraz à Bagdad, 1881-1882*, Phébus, 1990
Eastwick Richard, *The Gulistan: or Rose-garden of Shekh Muslihu'd-Din Sadi Shiraz*, Routledge, 2000
Faridani Nicol, *Iran*, Fahrang-Sara Publications, 1994
Ferdowsi, *Stories from the Shahnameh of Ferdowsi*, 3 volumes, Mage Publishers
Ghirshman Roman, *Iran: from the earliest times to the Islamic conquest*, Pelican, 1954
Ghirshman Roman, *Iran: Parthians and Sassanians*, Thames & Hudson, 1962
Godard André, *L'Art de l'Iran*, Arthaud, 1962
Gray Basil, *Persian Painting*, Macmillan, 1977
Hafez, *L'Amour, l'amant, l'aimé*, Sinbad, 1990
Hedayat S., *Trois Gouttes de sang*, Phébus, 1988
Hedayat S., *La Chouette aveugle*, J. Corti, 1988
Heuzé G., *Iran au fil des jours*, L'Harmattan, 1990
Hoag J., *Islamic Architecture*, Faber, 1987
Israel G., *Cyrus le Grand, fondateur de l'empire Perse*, Fayard, 1987
Izadpanah B., *Kerman*, Publication Organization of Ministry of Culture and Islamic Guidance
Journey, *A Passion for Iran*, Yassavoli Publications, 1998
Kasraian N. and Arshi Z., *Turkmans of Iran*, Seké Press, 1991
Kasraian N. and Arshi Z., *Kurds of Iran*, Seké Press, 1993
Kasraian N. and Arshi Z., *Our Homeland Iran*, Cheshmed Books Tehran, 1994
Kasraian N. and Arshi Z., *The South of Iran*, Leila Tavakoli first published, 1997
Khayyan Omar, *The Rubaiyat of Omar Khayyam*, Wordsworth Editions Ltd., 1996
Korbendau Yves, *L'Architecture sacrée de l'Islam*, A.C.R. Édition Paris Courbevoie, 1997
Loti Pierre, *Vers Ispahan*, Calman Lévy
Maheu René and Boissel Jean, *L'Iran, pérennité et rennaissance d'un empire*, Jeune Afrique, 1976
Massignen L. and Masse H., *L'Ame en Iran* (essai), Albin Michel, 1990
Morier James, *The Adventures of Hajji Baba of Ispahan*, Tynron Press, 1989
Porada Edith, *Ancient Iran*, Methuen, 1965
Pourafzal Hale and, Montgomery Roger, *The Spiritual Wisdom of Hafez: Teachings of the Philosopher of Love*, Inner Traditions International, 1998
Prince Ali Qadjar, *Les Rois oubliés, épopée de la dynastie qadjare*, Paris n°1, 1988
Rachet G., *Le Soleil de la Perse*, La table ronde, 1988
Richard Y., *L'Islam shi'ite*, Fayard, 1991
Saadu, *Le Jardin des roses*, Albin Michel, 1991
Sabahi T., *Splendeurs des tapis d'Orient*, Atlas, 1987
Safa Z. *Anthologie de la poésie persane (XIᵉ XIIᵉ siècle)*, Gallimard, 1987
Safari, *7 Climes of Iran*, Yassavoli Publications, 1998
Sinoué G., *Avicenne ou la route d'Ispahan*, Denoël, 1989
Stark Treya, *La Vallée des Assassins*, Voyageurs, Payot, 1991
Tavernier J.B., *Les Six Voyages en Turquie et en Perse*, La découverte, 1981
"Téhéran au dessous du volcan", Revue *Autrement* H.S. , 1987
Varenne J., *Zarathustra et la tradition mazdéenne*, Maîtres spirituels n° 35, Éd. du Seuil
Wearing Alison, *Honeymoon in Purdah*, Pan, 2001
Yassavoli Javas, *The Fabulous Iran*, Yassavoli Publications, 1994